T0129145

SEARCH FOR THE IMAGE OF
FOREFATHER
IN DREAMS

SEARCH FOR THE IMAGE OF
FOREFATHER
IN DREAMS

Among Former Bedouin Now Living in Town

GIDEON M. KRESSEL

Search for the Image of Forefather in Dreams
Among Former Bedouin Now Living in Town

iUniverse books may be ordered through booksellers or by contacting:

iUniverse
1663 Liberty Drive
Bloomington, IN 47403
www.iuniverse.com
1-800-Authors (1-800-288-4677)

ISBN: 978-1-4917-8828-8 (sc)
ISBN: 978-1-4917-8827-1 (e)

Library of Congress Control Number: 2016901317

Print information available on the last page.

iUniverse rev. date: 03/30/2016

Thank you for the three photos to Mr. Klaus-Otto Hundt.
Edited by Ms. Joan Hooper.

Contents

FOREWORD

Allah's Special Medicine: Dreaming about the Forefather among former Bedouin now living in town

By Nancy Hartevelt Kobrin, Ph.D.*

This work expresses the importance of the sheikhs' appearance in dreams as they appear in the dreams of Bedouin. Their purpose provides an unconscious meaning from the dreamer to the collective unconscious of the group. The dreams are viewed as a means of providing soothing, meaning and purpose to the group, mainly movement from archaic to modernity.

As a psychoanalyst I read with particular interest Professor Kressel's astute and sensitive analysis concerning the appearance of sheikhs in dreams where they appear to the dreamer as an archetypal father figure as a wish or fantasy for tribal unification, stability and solidarity. The dreamer who unconsciously has generated the sheikh image has arrived at

* Dr. Nancy Hartevelt Kobrin is a post-modern psychoanalyst whose doctorate focused on Al Andalus, aljamía (Old Spanish in Arabic script), communal identity formation and its relationship to the coexistence of the three Abrahamic faiths, prior to her training at the Chicago Institute of Psychoanalysis. She then became an expert on post-traumatic stress disorder and from there entered into the field of counter terrorism studies, developing a theory of imagery to explain the unconscious communication of the Islamic suicide attack.

a time of transition from rural to urban life for the dreamer. This is a time of great duress which is further complicated by being an Arab Muslim minority within a Jewish nation-state along with many other social issues such as worrying about being a provider, seeking a new career, bringing children into the world in order to appease elder group pressure, etc. These worries and stresses are intimately linked to the dream, which deals with the most intense human emotions such as jealousy, envy, shame, victimization and rage. Even though Allah was not a psychiatrist, as one woman quipped, the dream is "a dose of medicine" from Allah.

Like Professor Kressel I too had been drawn to Arabic and specifically al-jamía, Old Spanish written in Arabic script, preceding my training as a psychoanalyst. The extensive field work which Professor Kressel carried out brought back memories of my doctoral "field work" concerning another Muslim group, the Moriscos of medieval Spain, whose solidarity was under duress as they were forced to convert to Catholicism and who were ultimately expelled beginning in 1609. While I could only know these Muslims through the 16th century manuscripts that their scribes left behind, I came to feel close to them, spending long hours poring over scribes' handwriting. I felt that if I had walked through the market place in Spain, I could have recognized the scribe by his handwriting. My intimacy with them did not compare to the intense interpersonal relations that Professor Kressel developed in Jawârish that lead them to confide in him their precious dreams. Here, though as a psychoanalyst who loved listening to my patients' dreams and who has a certain penchant for Islam and Arabic culture, I felt a similar connection reading Professor Kressel's interpretation of their dreams.

My reading of this evocative work reminded me of the English expression we often use for people who intuitively think psychoanalytically. We say -- "If you walk like a duck and talk like a duck, you are a duck." There is no question that Professor Kressel is a consummate anthropological psychoanalyst. He had the unique opportunity to study psychoanalysis as a student while at the University of California Los Angeles. Professor Kressel's teachers were his aunt Dr. R. Schärf-Kluger and uncle Dr. Y.H. Kluger who brought Jungian analysis to Israel. By his fine attunement, interpersonal skills, the capacity to listen closely and respond in a non-shaming manner he is able to tap into the group psyche of the Bedouin. In truth, he has been doing this for years. Fortunately for us he saved all his notebooks from fieldwork done over forty years ago in the neighborhood of Jawârish in Ramle. The dreams are a cornerstone of this rich repository.

The Role of the Tribe
It is important to first recall that life in a desert society is very harsh. The individual cannot live apart from the group, the tribe or clan. The Bedouin developed a special way of dealing with that harsh reality through its group structure and the unique place of honor given to its forefathers. Dependency on one another is key as well as remembering their ancestors in order to bolster a sense of honor and pride. Thus commemorating the archetypes of the agnate by invoking their memory helps to solidify the group particularly during times of crisis, such as under the impact of urbanization. Hence the tribe has long served as the backbone of political negotiations and interpersonal affairs. Thus, its leader, the sheikh and his image function in the collective intrapsychic unconscious. The sheikh is considered to be the key figure on earth after Allah.

The Group Self, Shame and Fusion
Group psychology helps us understand group behavior, for instance how in the West the individual mind is more dominant and salient than the group mind of more repressive cultures such as the tribe or clan. This is important to keep in mind since Professor Kressel argues that the appearance of the

sheikh image in a dream is not so much a statement concerning the personal psyche of an individual but rather concerning the "dreamer's paternal kinship group" (p. 1). He focuses on something very important to which most Westerns might be blind, mainly the cultural and psychic life of the Bedouin.

Thus, the Bedouin mind is dominated more by a group self which is, indeed, more important as opposed to the individual self-prevalent in Western cultures. Theirs is a shame honor culture. Shame is a powerful tool to keep the group fused together emotionally. Its counterpart in the dream is the sheikh image, which helps to assuage the pervasiveness of being preoccupied by feeling and being shamed. The sheikh image helps the dreamer sort out his distress, being torn between developing a modern more individuated self apart from the group, yet remaining healthily linked to the group in a new and different way.

These groups remain largely fixated on shame/blame/honor, whereby to save face becomes a more pervasive force than life itself. At this vortex the boundaries become fused, making it unclear where culture, politics and personal boundaries exist and interface. It is well known in the psychological literature that shame in Western child rearing practices impedes the healthy development of the personality. It is all the more complicated in a shame honor culture such as the Bedouin because shame has become "ritualized" and hence "normalized" even though it is counter-productive to child development. Indeed it could be surmised that the Bedouin suffer from chronic shaming practices experienced during early childhood. DeYoung[1] as

---

[1] Patricia DeYoung (2015). *Understanding and Treating Chronic Shame: A Relational/Neurobiological Approach.* See also Judith Herman, "Shattered Shame States and Their Repair," http://www.challiance.org/Resource.ashx?sn=VOVShattered20ShameJ Herman, accessed 21 March 2015.

well as Herman have underscored the impact of shaming and its attendant problems in the interpersonal realm. [2]

Professor Kressel is right to claim that the dreamer, no matter if male or female, will both yearn for the appearance of the sheikh in dreaming rather than that of a grandmother. The sheikh simply carries more authority and weight and serves as a sign of hope for clarifying the dreamer's current predicament, which involves stresses of a modern urban life. The sheikh, then, becomes a wise and knowledge guide, helping the dreamer transition from rural to modern life.

The individual's dream is nonetheless embedded in the group self and forms a web of the relatives' relationship as a highly fused kinship. Fusion is a concept I borrow from Margaret Mahler.[3] She developed the notion of the maternal symbiosis where the infant perceives himself as one unit with the mother, undifferentiated. In shame honor cultures one grows into adulthood but remains fused to the mother and in turn all other relationships also remain highly fused. It is an internal struggle to become independent. In Arab Muslim culture such as the Bedouin, the bond between mother and child is "unseverable," according to the psychiatrist Dr. Sami Timimi.[4] The Pakistani Muslim psychiatrist psychoanalyst, Dr. Salman

---

[2] I hasten to add, based on my experience and extensive work with Middle East Studies scholars, Arabists, including scholars of Central Asia and counter terrorist experts, that while they may be well versed on the subject of shame honor cultures, they generally do not understand the deep ramifications of shaming practices as they are not trained in child development. This creates a blind spot. Fortunately Professor Kressel is an exception to my experience concerning the vital subject of shaming practices.

[3] Mahler, Margaret (2000). *The Psychological Birth of the Human Infant Symbiosis and Individuation,*

[4] Timimi, Sami (2002). *Pathological Child Psychiatry and the Medicalization of Childhood*, p. 22.

Akhtar, in many of his writings, has stressed the nature of dislocation experienced in immigration and even migration from rural to urban. The trauma concerns loss of the sense of group self-cohesion entailing mourning and adaptation in one's new environment.[5]

So how does this fit with the appearance of the sheikh in dreams? The sheikh image acts as a bridging mechanism from the contemporary urban present to the ancient past, as he is the most charismatic figure to mobilize group behavior. Roland (1998) highlights the struggle for the non-Western self who remains in closer interdependent relationships. This self nearly always needs psychological reinforcement from the group, especially its leaders. This resonates with the dreamer seeking approval from the interpreter by bringing a dream image of the sheikh, a dream of great importance. Thus, the dream can be thought of as having a kind of voice of its own that transmits unconsciously messages to the dreamer through the dream interpreter.

By focusing on this paternal aspect of kinship, the sheikh image bolsters the group fantasy of solidarity. The female is also present but remains devalued. The institutionalization of the valued first-born male is in opposition to the devalued baby girl. The female can be seen only behind the scenes unconsciously as a background object of support and fusion for the male. The female's raison de être is to bring male babies into the world for honor. Since the male baby is the female's narcissistic object of honor, the baby is never permitted to separate from his mother. The female is not seen as a "whole object," existing solely as a part object mainly for the purpose of the 'ird, the locus of familial honor, i.e., her pelvis.

---

[5]   Akhtar, Salman (2011). *Immigration and Acculturation: Mourning, Adaptation and the Next Generation.*

Ironically, the female then is tantamount to keeping the entire paternal kinship group enterprise functioning, though this remains unspoken and part of the unconscious infrastructure for the group self. Most likely this could never really be admitted consciously, so it goes undercover behind the veil. To admit to this would bring shame to the group. Therefore, it is inconceivable that there could be a female counterpart to a sheikh. Furthermore, her unspoken power resides in the scientific fact that she builds the brain of the baby in utero, until age three when it triples in size. Building the brain of the baby is significant because neuroscience now tells us that this is the time frame when a baby acquires empathy through the development of mirror neurons.[6] There is some thought too that the building blocks for morality are also acquired at this time.[7] Both empathy and morality are needed in order to move out of a shame honor culture into a more nonviolent environment where honor does not have to be regained by willfully spilling blood. Hence, the devalued female, who is the unconscious shock absorber of rage for the patriarchal tribe, clan, *hamula*, etc., is working at a disadvantage. These are not optimal conditions for maternal attachment for mother and baby. She is building the baby's brain living under a death threat. We can speculate that the stress hormones are significant and the annihilation anxiety runs high. The baby is at risk of not developing empathy, or a sense of intimacy. Mother as cultural interpreter unconsciously communicates the unspoken rules of the tribe, namely power, control and submission are substitutes for intimacy. We surmise that this repeats the cycle, contributing to violence. None of this is to blame the mother because after all she was the devalued

---

[6] Marco Iacoboni (2009). *Mirroring People: The Science of Empathy and How We Connect with Others.*

[7] Aner Govrin. "The ABC of Moral Development," *Frontiers of Psychology,* 2014; 5: 6, http://www.ncbi.nlm.nih.gov/pmc/articles/PMC3901400/, accessed 21 March 2015.

little girl; rather this is the scientific reality of the crux of the cultural problem.

Under Threat of Fragmentation of the Group Self

With the impact of modernization and migration to the city, the group self is threatened both internally and externally with fragmentation and lack of cohesion. Will the Bedouin community lose its group self? Will assimilation take place?

As Professor Kressel has noted the Bedouin family that moves to an urban setting is under considerable unspoken psychological pressures as the solidarity of the group is called into question, i.e., the nature of their social nest. Will the sheikh lose his power as the women become more modernized and move outside the grip of the tightly bound patriarchal environment?

The image of the sheikh in the dream also offers itself as a psychological link to this attachment. Even though its precursor in attachment remains the "hidden" early mother, the male is able to reassert himself. Relocation from rural to urban would initially precipitate a psychological regression of sorts. This fits with Professor Kressel's assertion that the dreams are a return to "an ancient social order" (p. 20). I merely suggest that this ancient social order can also be read in light of the maternal. Reminiscent of nesting dolls, the paternal agnate archetypal structure has an inner core of maternal attachment, which mediates the agnate. The bitter paradox is no matter how hard they try, they cannot escape the importance of the mother.

The Significance of the Group Tie to the Agnate

The formalized paternal lineage provides the known psychological infrastructure for the group self. Within these cultures remains oral tradition, which maintains a collective memory of paternal kinship, valued and passed on from one generation to the next through its memorization. The recitation of the dream can be considered as an extension of this oral tradition. The delicate fragile nature of the shame honor group self is clearly understood by Professor Kressel. An outsider might not be so aware of the sensitivities of the male ego living under the pervasive law of a shame honor culture. The glue of the group self is the historical link to the agnate. Professor Kressel intuitively steers clear of interpreting the "maternal" as that would be "too close to home." Such an interpretation would be experienced as shaming. It would also miss the importance of the agnate tie.

In addition there is another inherent, unspoken paradox as the sheikh was once himself a little boy who never psychologically separated from his mother. She changes her name to that of his. The mother "weds" herself to her firstborn male and by extension his agnate. Just as the sheikh is experienced as a father image and hence authoritarian, he nevertheless ironically remains a symptom of the underlying problem -- the devalued female. The family is the microcosm of society.[8] Therefore, the image of the forefather in dreams articulates the unconscious communication to the entire male dominated group. Professor Kressel writes:

"Unlike the commotion surrounding the Oedipal Complex, focusing on parents-offspring, mother-son and father-daughter psychological complexes, the bond of an arch-forefather that obligates his descendent generations, all men, to guarantee one another's offence-defense complications gained less attention. Looking at causes of empathy and antipathy among agnates, often out of the group's *over-engagement* [emphasis mine] with its members' intimate affairs, intense commitments to one another and their common tribal descent has drawn much less on psychological concern. A modern philosophy of life accentuates individuality and plays down ancient perceptions

---

[8]   Barakat, Halim (1993). *The Arab World Society Culture and State.*

that once bound us and committed us to serving our groups of descent and their cause, even if they were wrong" (p. 22).

Professor Kressel goes on to cite the important work of Jung concerning the image of the Mother Archetype. She does appear in dreams but her meaning is different where emphasis is on "goodness, passion and darkness"(p. 11, citing Jung, pp. 15-44.) In counterpoint he stresses Jung's observation that the paternal archetype in dreams is a figure which looks out for and protects the kin in order for the group to survive, emphasized above as the harshness of desert culture.

Pondering My "Archetypal" Genetic Maternal Kinship
Inevitably I found myself reflecting on my own links to the past, my own ancestral landscape. I have a special interest in the intersection of our genetic makeup, human evolution in conjunction with our fantasies about our ancestral past.[9] Six years ago I went one step further and did DNA testing through National Geographic's genome project.[10]

After taking a cheek swab and waiting six weeks, National Geographic sent me a map of my maternal DNA reaching back 150,000 years. According to their findings, I had walked out of Namibia straight north through Israel, proceeding northward to Finland. I had not told National Geographic that I was Jewish. Astoundingly, their report revealed too that inscribed into my DNA were three of the "genetic" Jewish mothers out

---

[9] See also *Ancestral Landscapes in Human Evolution: Culture, Childrearing and Social Wellbeing* (2014).

[10] http://shop.nationalgeographic.com/ngs/browse/productDetail. jsp?productId=2001246&gsk&code=SR90004&keyword =national+geographic+genome+project&OVMTC=Exact&site =&creative=34441970777&OVKEY=national%20geograp hic%20genome%20project&url_id=120324817&adpos=1t1&de vice=c&gclid=CJS-iZbAuMICFUoUwwodr4MAPA

of four. This experience took me farther back in time than simply limiting my thoughts and fantasies to my Dutch Jewish paternal surname Hartevelt and my Rumanian/Hungarian Jewish maternal surname Kandel vis-à-vis my genealogy. Having been impressed by Ann Ancelin Schutzenberger's *The Ancestor Syndrome: Transgenerational Psychotherapy and the Hidden Links of the Family Tree*[11] I could not help wonder about my own ancestors.

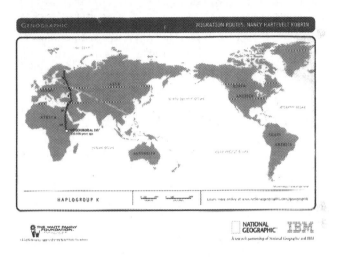

More associations and commonalities came to mind concerning continuity across generations, linking life to death and our mortality. One dreamer related how he missed his grandfather and in turn this kindled reminiscences for Professor Kressel and in turn for me as well. I never had the opportunity to know either one of my grandfathers though I had many fantasies about them as pillars in my life, a source of stability and strength. They had fleetingly appeared in dreams and perhaps they were "my sheikhs."

---

[11] Schutzenberger also founded the field of psychodrama.

Who were my ancestors? What were my "memes" – those ideas, which had been passed on to me, "the cultural equivalent of a gene, the basic element of biological inheritance" (p. 35). What was my paternal kinship group like as I along with my maternal DNA trudged over the same geographic area as these Bedouin dreamers? I wondered, might we even have relatives in common besides Abraham, Sarah and Hagar? How did this intergenerational unconscious communication manifest itself in me as a dreamer? What might be the intersection between genes, epigenetics, child rearing practices and the modeling of life experience through the group?[12] Professor Kressel's work raised a plethora of questions. Look how Abraham gave importance to Sara who immediately banished Ishmael and his mother to the desert. Thus the Jewish mother!

Uncannily, I too immigrated back to that same spot on the map where these dreamers live. The DNA map merely confirmed my unconscious ties to my forefathers and foremothers. It made sense to me that a person's dream is an indicator for the entire group. Dreams are to be shared because it is a fused group unlike in a Western environment where the dream is brought to the therapist to be interpreted.

Jawârish Today
Another irony abound. My partner and I visited Ramle over two years before I was invited to share my thoughts about Professor Kressel's interpretation of dreams. Reading that the dreams came from members of this particular neighborhood

---

[12] For a wonderful interview with Rachel Yehuda, a psychiatrist and neuroscientist, Do Jews Carry Trauma in Our Genes? A Conversation With Rachel Yehuda.
The innovative neuroscientist discusses how the Holocaust, famine, and other catastrophic experiences can affect our DNA, see http://tabletmag.com/jewish-arts-and-culture/books/187555/trauma-genes-q-a-rachel-yehuda, accessed 11 December 2014.

caused me to reflect on what has changed. I had never been to Jawârish before immigrating to Israel in 2010 so I did not know Jawârish of forty years ago when Professor Kressel did his intensive fieldwork. Now it seemed the neighborhood had become more polarized and the neighborhood had become off limits to Jews. Unfortunately the name "Jawârish" has become synonymous with violence, crime and drugs. A Mafioso like feeling pervaded the air. We did not venture in. It was not safe and this was my partner's assessment, all the more striking since his expertise is the Israeli Arab minority. I wondered if it would even be possible to undertake such anthropological fieldwork today. I rather doubt it. For this reason alone Professor Kressel's observations and analysis are extremely important.

The Dreamer's Narcissism and the Dream as Transitional Object
From maternal DNA to reflections on Jawârish, the dreams evoked an intruding sense of modernity. The issue of individuality surfaced in the dreamer's narcissism. To share his or her dream with a non-member of the agnate, Professor Kressel, must be viewed as a new experience of modern life for Bedouin culture. Professor Kressel correctly noted the special attention the dreamer would receive in the telling of the dream. To stand out in such a fused group is unusual as one is suppose to blend in for the sake of group solidarity. Indeed, it strikes a modern perspective of the self. We can assume that Professor Kressel held a unique sense of trust, which was further enhanced by his empathic listening, which must have been a new experience for the Bedouin, hence holding the potential for change and adaptation. The dreamer momentarily would step into the group limelight, becoming "special," presenting his dream of the sheikh as a unique gift to both Professor Kressel as well as his group. The dream's precious gift held the means of improving group relations. The dynamic of specialness is a narcissistic trait as opposed to

those seeking to attach or to prove their existence as seen in borderline self-states.

I came to think of these dreams in particular as a unique genre bridging life and death, a dream as a transitional object offering structure for a self under duress of urbanization. The psychological terms – self-soothing object and its function – came to mind. The sense of mortality changes with urbanization. One tends to be more alone and isolated, evocative of mortality. However, since this set of dreams invokes the archetype of the agnate, it functions to link the dreamer to his tribe's ancient past. Islam does not adhere to worshipping graven images of Allah so that the appearance of a sheikh in a dream acts as a bridging mechanism to Allah. "The general pattern in which Sheikhs appear followed an old-fashion prototype. Somewhere in my text [writes Kressel] I added the words that Sheikhs are expected to return the way the Messiah is awaited among the Jews."

While I was reading about all of the dreams it was at this point that the Arabic adage popped into my head that "Heaven lies under the feet of the mother." Life begins with mother but ends with Allah. The telling of the dream compliments the oral tradition. The dream evoked a modern means of re-enforcing tribal affiliations.

Professor Kressel writes: "Psychoanalysts rightly favor evaluating their clients' problems against their immediate family and primary relations. Relatives of the first degree affect our feelings and therefore influence our behavior more than the distant ones, and the nuclear family nest is to be looked at before all distant relations. On the other hand it is part of the social reality in the Middle East that draws attention to *'umûm* (paternal relatives) and to *ikhwâl* (maternal relatives) in different ways. The issues of tribes and of tribal ascription of clients are here of particular relevance and not only in the capacity of background detail. Knowing the potential of agnate even of a distant order to appear at once *as if* [emphasis mine] they were of first degree ones, when certain circumstances occur, requires caution. Susceptible to be drawn closer are chiefly *'umûm*. Rarely do *ikhwâl* come to fulfill these roles. Observing the tribe and the extended family setup alone and discovering that deep roots of paternal ascription affect the individual psyche are liable to affect one's type of dreams" (p. 24).

Madame Khamisah the Consummate Bedouin Analyst

I would like to conclude with an example of how the maternal subtly functions in such a male dominated environment. I focus on Madame Khamisah. Professor Kressel introduces us to her at the very beginning of his work. He calls Madame Khamisah Abu Kashef a "knowing woman" as he draws us into the lives of the Bedouin community. We could consider her the equivalent of a psychoanalytic mother analyst. All different kinds of people would seek her out to enhance their knowledge. Unconsciously they would momentarily return to their maternal attachment. She would not ask out right – "what are your problems," rather, like a finely attuned therapist she would begin her meeting by reading the person's coffee cup. To be direct would be shaming. Thus, she also did not stare or engage the eyes – this would be too shaming and too intense, especially given the fact that the culture is imbued with the notion of the evil eye. Professor Kressel refers to the "evil eye" and joins it with the feeling of jealousy, suggesting then that this is a community that feels itself to be under surveillance.

Madame Khamisah intuitively would read the client's "personal weather report" about how he was feeling. Perhaps Madame Khamisah Abu Kashef was someone easier to relate to because we are told about her husband's facial birth defect, a cleft lip and the fact that she was married off late in life, childless and black, holding a lower social status. I viewed this odd couple as one. Remarkably, many years ago early in my clinical practice, I wound up receiving a number of referrals of individuals with this particular facial trauma. I was even elected to the American Cleft Palate-Cranial Facial Association. My patients were all acutely and remarkably gifted in reading other people's nonverbal communication, especially facial expression.

I reflected back on my patients while associating to the related subject of leaders with a defect. They have a peculiar charisma for their followers who unconsciously project on to them (such as Madame Khamisah and her husband) their sense of defectiveness, their own imperfections, their shame. By doing so they feel themselves pure and empowered. Schiffer wrote extensively about the leader with a defect in *Charisma: A Psychoanalytic Look at Mass Society*. As resident dream analyst Madame Khamisah had impressive intuitive abilities. "She grew to fulfill the office of an analyst by knowing how to listen and then approaching her client's problem gently" (p. 27). No doubt Heinz Kohut, the founder of Self Psychology, would have described her as a gentle selfobject for the patient, meaning that these dreamers could attach themselves to her unconsciously and feel supported in their time of crisis.

Indeed Professor Kressel stresses, "Social change does not occur suddenly. Keen observation of urbanization throughout the Middle East and in comparison to these processes elsewhere indicate the lasting hold of pre-urban patterns of association" (p. 33). From my clinical experience I also recalled how seemingly modern families could still adhere to very old traditionally ingrained attitudes and tendencies. Change also came very slowly for the patients.

Thus the image of the Sheikh's appearance in dreams of Bedouin preserves a special link to the past while allowing for the evolution of the group self as it slowly eases into modernity. Forty years ago Professor Kressel's fieldwork and notebooks inscribed this arduous process of transition through intuitively collecting these dreams about sheikhs and the agnate. The dream is viewed here as offering both a transitional space and a needed object for self-soothing for the group under duress as well as the dreamer. There is much pride and honor when a sheikh appears in one's dream. I wondered in turn as I concluded this reading, which of my ancestors may have known their forefathers and might a sheikh visit me in a future dream as well? After all we are more alike than we are different.

Bibliography

Ancestral Landscapes in Human Evolution: Culture, Childrearing and Social Wellbeing (2014). Ed. D. Narvaez, K. Valentino, A. Fuentes, J. J. McKenna and P. Gray. New York: Oxford University Press.

Akhtar, Salman (2011). *Immigration and Acculturation: Mourning, Adaptation and the Next Generation*. New York: Jason Aronson.

Barakat, Halim (1993). *The Arab World Society Culture and State*. Berkeley and Los Angeles: The University of California Press.

Dundes, Alan (1992). *The Evil Eye: A Casebook*. Madison: University of Wisconsin.

Iacoboni, Marco (2009). *Mirroring People: The Science of Empathy and How We Connect with Others*. New York: Picador.

Kobrin, Nancy Hartevelt (2010). *The Banality of Suicide Terrorism: The Naked Truth About Islamic Suicide Bombing*. Washington, D.C.: Potomac. See also Hebrew edition with foreword by Professor Gideon Kressel (2012) New Rochelle, New Jersey: MultiEducator.

_____ (2013). *Penetrating the Terrorist Psyche*. New Rochelle, New Jersey: MultiEducator.

_____ (2014). *The Maternal Drama of the Chechen Jihadi*. Washington, D.C.: Jason Aronson. www.freepsychotherapy book.org and print on demand. New Rochelle, New Jersey: MultiEducator.

Mahler, Margaret (2000). *The Psychological Birth of the Human Infant: Symbiosis and Individuation*. New York: Basic Books.

Roland, Alan (1998). *In Search of Self in India and Japan: Toward a Cross-Cultural Psychology*. Princeton, N.J.: Princeton University Press.

Schiffer, Irving (1974). *Charisma: A Psychoanalytic Look at Mass Society*. Toronto: University of Toronto Press and the Free Press.

Schutzenberger, Anne Anecelin (1998). *The Ancestor Syndrome: Transgenerational Psychotherapy and the Hidden Links of the Family Tree*. New York: Routledge.

Timimi, Sami (2002). *Pathological Child Psychiatry and the Medicalization of Childhood*. New York: Brunner-Routledge.

Internet

Do Jews Carry Trauma in Our Genes? A Conversation With Rachel Yehuda. The innovative neuroscientist discusses how the Holocaust, famine, and other catastrophic experiences can affect our DNA, see http://tabletmag.com/jewish-arts-and-culture/books/187555/trauma-genes-q-a-rachel-yehuda, accessed 11 December 2014.

Govrin, Aner. "The ABC of Moral Development," *Frontiers of Psychology*, 24 January 2014, http://www.ncbi.nlm.nih.gov/pmc/articles/PMC3901400/, accessed 21 March 2015.

Herman, Judith. "Shattered Shame States and their Repair," http://www.challiance.org/Resource.ashx?sn=VOVShattered 20ShameJHerman, accessed 21 March 2015.

National Geographic Genome Project, http://shop.nationalgeographic.com/ngs/browse/productDetail.jsp?productId=2001246&gsk&code=SR90004&keyword=national+geographic+genome project&OVMTC=Exact&site=&creative=34441970777&OVKEY=national%20geographic%20genome%20project&url id=120324817&adpos=1t1&device=c&gclid=CJS-iZbAuMICFUoUwwodr4MAPA

PREFACE

Dreams of mystic experiences may suggest an action in which the spectator becomes involved. However, impressive dreams may have no lasting or transformative affect on the dreamer. Being impressed by one's own dream in a capacity of an on-looking outsider does not necessarily signify a personal problem. The cases in this study do not engage the dreamers in a personal manner as much as they concern the dreamer's paternal kinship group. Noting that specific dreams capture public attention, they are related to one's senior agnates and comprehended by them with particular care. Viewed as meant for awakening group awareness, a dream can be taken as source material that carries a collective message of importance for the group as a whole. This study's puzzle is the logic by which an individual's dream may engage the dreamer's relatives and thus contain a revelation for them jointly.

At the same time, the world of dreams and the experience of ecstasy (ekstasis) can be seen as "standing" or "stepping" outside reality, as it is commonly defined. Ecstasy transcends the world of everyday life. Manifest experience retains its primary status in consciousness. The precariousness of a world made up of "facts" is revealed any time we forget or doubt our facts of life. Questioning our present existence leads to a tendency of resorting to dreams, all the more so to acknowledge them as a "part of reality," even when they collide with the truth of daylight.

Truth that becomes apparent to us while we are asleep is at times viewed as a correcting one that comes to question our objectivity. Then we tend to embrace dreams as part of an objective truth, and not as an expression of madness. All the more so when we consciously encounter death and contemplate a way out of its cycle, as an outlet that embraces the idea of an afterlife. To an extent, we tend to acknowledge the intervention of individuals belonging to our predecessor generations as though they are on guard ready to intervene in our life, to retain for our joint interest a measure of eternal truth.

In the cases dealt with in the following, descendents of once nomadic pastoralists (Bedouin) now living in town have dreams in which one of their ancient forefathers appears. When an old paternal Sheikh appears in a dream, the belief is that his goal is to employ the dreamer as a harbinger who is to pass on a divine pronouncement to warn his or her living relatives.

A common belief has it that a dream may bear a message, designed by the Divine and planted in a person, a woman or a man, to be brought to the knowledge of his or her paternal group mates. The belief here is that the Almighty chooses this cover to approach people he trusts and selects for a mission — while they are asleep, who are to spread what he has to say among their paternal relatives. Dreams are sought and expected to arrive wrapped up and mixed with various side views, seemingly not related to one another, or even different in kind. These elements need to be filtered out or peeled away in order to place the less important aside.

Allah's sayings are often disguised, not employing the daily vernacular used by the people engaged as an indicative sign.

Frequently Allah decorates sights shown to dreamers with elements that make them hard to interpret, but after all, familiar to the few people who know and can "open dreams by means like the coffee cup test."[13] Clues in dreams are often intuitively professional; once they appear, mixed though relevant, the more experienced family members are brought to think about them because the insight wrapped in them provides consequences that influence the entire group. Dreams that touch on only private matters are left alone, that is, left to be personal and remain unnoticed by the dreamer's (agnatic) relatives.

---

[13] *Illy byeftahu b-al finjân.le*

AGNATION

Where herdsmen are led by Sheikhs, who are their paternal elders, heads of their family groups, they follow an enduring tradition. Fathers' fathers' fathers represent the passing generations of Sheikhs who were the tribe's leaders ever since it came into being. Present-day leaders of tribes follow the millennia-old track that relates ascription to semen alone. New groups of men appeared at a certain moment in history to annul the genetic significance of the ovum in favor of semen. Inheritance thus came to be seen as ascribed to fathers and the fetus as belonging to its begetting male. Since then groups are ascribed by blood via semen. Semen is equated to seeds placed in the ground, thus, the ear of corn belongs to the person who sows, not to the "motherland" into which it came into being (Delaney, 1987).

Paternal kinship groups emerged in various parts of the ancient world among people who adjusted themselves anew in the struggle for existence. On being forced to start producing food, societies that had been organized for hunting and food gathering had to change their habits. Adjusting to Holocene climatic conditions necessitated reshaping man's patterns of groupings as well. This occurred along with two different lines: farming and herding. Farming gave rise to the extended family group while shepherding evolved along with tribal groups. A tribal form evolved in areas of savanna, first along with shepherding in various parts of the Asian steppes. Semi-desert lands where precipitation did not provide sufficient water, not even for dry farming, provided the setting at which herding societies emerged.

Making a living from breeding livestock led to herding or, alternatively, growing fodder for them. Herding was less strenuous and by far cheaper, but it obliged the wandering about with herds in search of pasture. New types of homes were designed for this purpose, to enable the dismantling of the "home" and loading it on backs of camels. New patterns of social adaptation were needed as well, to look after the herds lest rivals would steal them when isolated in distant herding grounds. When allies for mutual security were needed, to pursue thieves and bring one's herds back, the tribe came into being.

Tribal organizations gave leverage to relatively small groups of herders over massive groups of sedentary folk (Sahlins, 1961), either peasant or urban. The nomads' means of securing pasture could be employed as well vis-à-vis sedentary people. By joining forces, nomads could fall on sleepy villages and towns, one after the other. Not being bound to a piece of land enabled the herders to move over long distances in search of a living.

Desertification processes made the cultivation of prairie plots risky; using them for pasture could still be practical. At the same time herds could make use of fields of stubble through agreements with farmers. Pasture on sown fields and plantations, disregarding the farmers' protests and attempts to fight back, occurred mainly where peasant communities were isolated. When state organs failed to restore stolen property from their desert hideaways, farmers went bankrupt.

The more herders were aggravated by constraints of climate and drought, the more pressure they put on the sedentary population. Frequent scarcity of rains pushed herders and herds into the watered, cultivated valleys. Clashes between them and the farming communities could not be avoided. Only powerful, well-organized and well-equipped armies could stand by, protecting villages and their sown fields, pushing intruders away.

State armies, once weakened, lost to herding tribes. Sheikhs had the upper hand and a byproduct of their triumph meant that the tribal system began to appear among peasants and urban societies throughout the Middle East cultural area. Herders turned for the most part northward, from the dry steppes of the Sahara in the West throughout the Southern Middle East, reaching Mesopotamia in the East. Herding tribes that led their animals into the sown areas had the option of turning to farming, i.e., forsaking the desert and the idea of shepherding for good. Alternative sources of income were sought.

One of these alternative sources of income, aside from breeding herds and modest attempts at agriculture, was taxing the sedentary population. Stationary herders on the verges of farming lands raised "fraternity" money called *khuwa* or *khuwa*, meaning "brotherhood fee," to help them protect the vegetation from harm caused by herds. Peasant communities thus supported guarding the fields (Eph'al, 1982).

The flow of Bedouin tribes turned largely north and west via the Hejaz in the northwestern part of the Arabian Peninsula. Most tribes found their way to the Nile Valley. Many of them moved further west along the North African shore, reaching the Atlantic Ocean and the Iberian Peninsula. Massive migration of tribes out of Arabia occurred after the 7th century, such as the migration of Bani Sulaym and Bani Hilal in the 11th century, a massive move that took them westward (Ronart, 1959), reaching the Maghreb.

Muslims who travelled to Arabia following the *Hajj* commandment and devout pilgrims (*Hujjuj*) who arrived in Mecca time and again, either for the sake of *'Umra* (visiting the

Ka'aba at any time of the year save for the Hajj time) enriched the hosting infrastructure. All of these visitors made up for the loss of livestock, thus saving Arabia's economy before the discovery of oil fields. The holy cities still provide a great share of the Saudi GNP, although not as much as that provided by oil.

A "tribe" is an aggregation of families related to one another by virtue of their fathers' descent from one man's seed. A common stock gives them a reason to act under the central authority of a male chief, and therefore attain joint political and economic objectives. Ruled by a patrilineal criterion, this set up gives men the dominant say in all tribal concerns.

Following a position held in the more distant past, tribes were first thought to have been breeding units, i.e., groups of people who were the descendents of a female progenitor, a "great foremother," via her daughter's daughter's daughter, providing a female line of descent.

Processes of conglomeration gradually formed extended patrilineal family groups into larger unions that were the early tribes. The size of the unit determined its position, and the bigger it was, i.e., the greater the number of combatant men it could mobilize (Kressel, 1996), implied greater force and a higher position up the social ladder. The quantity of tribesmen symbolized quality. The more numerous the cohorts of men were on the day of confrontation, the better were the tribe's chances to win the battle and thus come out on top of the social ladder.

Among the sedentary peoples of those distant years, ranking followed different patterns. On the whole, rank was the effect of might in farming, crafts, trade and administration. Dwellers in villages and towns were by far greater in number relative to their Bedouin adversaries but they lacked a guiding hand, an authority to lead them cohesively into battle, a quality the Bedouin had by nature of their tribal composition. In order to confront and prevail over the Bedouin challengers the peasants were in need of a leader, an organizing factor in times of emergency. A charismatic leader, be he a judge, an officer or a clergyman, was needed when leadership was required.

Small groups of tribesmen led by Sheikhs could confront unorganized sedentary folk and have the upper hand. Since the middle of the 7th century, following the conquests of Islam, herders had gradually transmitted their tribal pattern of organization to all parts of the population. Thus, villagers and townsmen became increasingly tribal. Little by little all subdivided their dwelling quarters by virtue of ascription.

Tales beginning with Abel in the Bible relate the story of a primordial herder. Abel represents an occupation that must have appeared at about the same time as the domestication of livestock in the Near East lands. As an individual Abel was not associated with a tribe, yet he is understood to represent a social entity that existed in his time that challenged the sedentary portion of mankind. Rivalry has characterized the relationship between the two since earliest times. Later herders prevailed in the Near East as a whole and influenced the behavior of others, regardless of their tradition, place of residence or occupation.

From the time that tribal organization spread into the entire Near East, it represents one of the primary features as a salient physiognomy of this Cultural Area. Crystallization of **hamail** (sig. **hamulah**, patri-lateral extended family groups) and of tribes solidified in due time and appeared everywhere. Since then tribal identity typifies the subdivisions observed in towns and villages of the Mideast as a whole, until this day.

Over the last years disputes have led to bitter civil wars, drawn on tribal identity, ethnicity and creed (Shi'ah—Sunna). The current reason so often used by contemporary societies for a *casus belli* is erroneously thought of as material gain. On the contrary, wars incur an obvious price largely unjustified in terms of sectorial and national economy, all the more so, bringing about an awful waste, not to mention the price of lives.

Residual memory of the *Salafi* age accounts (first century of Islam), that was forsaken for fourteen hundred years and nearly forgotten by the successive Muslim generations, is currently being brought to mind and blows the flames of a glowing ember. Not a desire for material gain but vengeance per se is the driving force here. Ever since the growth of a tribal infrastructure of society, elements of the morality of blood feud have penetrated to affect a transformation of interpersonal into inter-group relationships, and cast a wide shadow over ordinary economic transactions.

In deserts where water is scarce and priceless, "blood is thicker [i.e., heavier] than water." A drop of blood can trigger revenge that can lead to a feud lasting years. The principle of revenge is endorsed by all, yet pertains to relatives of the paternal line, the *'ummum*, not the maternal relatives, *ikhwal*. Divisions of consanguine relatives by relatedness to father or mother grew first among shepherds, and then took over the sedentary population of the Near East as well.

According to Darwin's theory (1871) men began to rule the family group in some parts of the Old World due to a change of ecological conditions. Previously mothers lead their families and men, the fathers of their offspring were no more than fortuitous visitors. They belonged to their mothers' groups and were occasional guests of women nearby.

Bearing in mind that this phase of evolution in which motherhood was replaced as a source of ascription by paternity, bestowing respect onto a prime father, occurred following a climatic change, after the pluvial era and the spread of the Holocene weather conditions. In the quest for man's prehistoric origins agnation has been viewed as a later and therefore at that time a better fitting pattern of social organization, which replaced other, hypothetical, more primitive forms of existence (see Roheim, 1932, 1947; Smith, 1889).

In accordance with the premise that climate change was a prime mover, the earliest family groups appeared to move about in search of food. Mothers and their offspring, young and adult sons and daughters moved together. At that time family groups were by definition matri-focal and matrilineal.

Geological and archaeological traces of the "neolithic revolution" teach a story of continuous droughts and desertification as natural disasters that encouraged the appearance and spread of the father's right. By the time hunting (small game) and food gathering were replaced by farming and shepherding fathers took the lead and pulled the family group to follow their steps.

In fact, these two new patterns of adaptation occurred at one and the same time and both let fathers take the family lead. Farming began with domestication of wild flora. Shepherding came about alongside the domestication of livestock that has been related with husbandry. Agriculture required stability of families dependent on the soil and a system of cultivation. Soil has been connected with motherhood, communities requiring locations.

These earliest practices of food production emerged and remained fixed to banks of rivers and water sources. At the same time, herding occurred in the prairie, beyond areas of arable land, therefore encouraging nomadism. While farmers began to build homes, shepherds learned to weave tents, and fold them up and transfer their dwellings, following their herds' movement in search of sustenance.

The two patterns of food production evolved soon after the pluvial era and progressed during the Holocene, i.e., a recent and warmer time. The time of the dry climatic conditions emerged some ten thousand years ago (following the arguments first presented by the 19th century evolutionists. See Smith, 1885).

These different methods both required human work. Although dissimilar from one another, they shaped two kinds of social organization: irrigated farming led to peasant communities and pastoral nomadism gave rise to tribes.

Both occupations produced surplus sufficient to enable the two kinds of producers an exchange of products in peace, thus bargain and gain. However, this exchange between them could arouse disagreements and quarrels as well. Different estimations of price regarding the value of items each one of them offered implied a valuation of their occupations. Prior to articulation of the theories of price and hence the balance of supply and demand, professional pride nourished resentments when, e.g., a surplus of goods offered at the market place forced the price down.

With the balance of **work** in mind, the production of fruits and vegetable required more manual labor than herding. In fact, for both groups specialization helped increase skill, which enabled them, mutually, the production of surplus and reduction of prices of produce. At the same time this could promote disputes. Profiting from exchanges implied a feeling of being cheated, mostly on the side of the farmers. Encounters between traders, representatives of the two groups, exacerbated jealousy and hatred.

Although each society could bargain its surplus produces and gain, the flexibility of bargaining placed the farmer at a disadvantage. For example, fruits and vegetables had to be given away at the end of the market day while livestock could be taken home waiting for another day and a better price. The farmers felt they earned their living by hard work while the pastoral nomads were idle, wandering with their herds, no more.

In view of deals of barter exchange, the value of goods taken away by the shepherd, most commonly clothing, tools of all kinds, arms, food, mostly cereals, seemed by far more expensive than the items the peasants received in exchange, be it dairy products or mutton. Livestock could be raised on farms as well, although fed on fodder, which is more costly than natural pasture, but nevertheless emphasizes the farm's autarchy.

Indeed, Cain and Abel were brothers; nonetheless, upon maturing and living by way of their work, jealousy came between them. Hate kindled firstly on the side of the farmer towards the shepherd. The earliest representatives of the two occupations following the Neolithic Revolution were symbolized by the Genesis story of the second generation, offspring of Adam and Eve. Each of them stood for a quarter of mankind when one felt abused by his brother, and therefore made him a victim, murdered by the other, mercilessly.

Confronted with one another, the two primeval occupations formed, contrasted and lead by different sets of conventions and values. Yet, following the Genesis episode, murder was felt or sensed to be a sin, if not yet set by law, prior to any codex on earth. By intuition the ethics emerged before the eternal commandments were set down, no matter the circumstance. The threat of murder was thought to be an unforgivable crime millennia prior to the Ten Commandments and "Thou Shall Not Kill." Cain and Abel were expected to deal with one another with understanding and reach a suitable agreement, and remain brothers in flesh and in spirit as well. What actually nourishes rivalry the Bible leaves to the imagination.

Food gathering came to an end in most parts of the Middle East and in other parts of the world when precipitation dwindled and forced mankind "out of Paradise." People began to produce food as though punished to do so, following the Divine Command: "**by the sweat of thy brow shalt thou eat bread.**"

Production rather than collection of food had a further impact on growth and development of society. Farming societies, mostly those dependent on harnessing of river water for irrigation of fields, needed collaboration. The need of an overall rule, monitored by inspectors, gave rise to kingdoms. Based on collection of taxes, kings built their luxurious palaces. Peasants were mobilized for compulsory labor service; in times of need to dig or clean canals of silt, men were forcibly taken from their homes.

Farm work could be run in part by women, but not so the handling of livestock. The herding of livestock, camels, cattle and sheep, was the responsibility of men. Among herders, every stranger encountered in the desert was a suspected enemy. Personal safety and that of the herd depended on men's strength and the concern that the tribe would avenge any spilled blood.

The more the economy turned to the production of food it became controlled by men and defense became essential, the role of men determined the position of their family group, and the social composition altered to favor them. Families became patri-local and patrilineal accordingly. Men's dominance shaped the social infrastructure anew in favor of paternal tribes. Herding societies seem to transform earliest with great zeal. However, both farming and shepherding societies reached a point at which men took the lead in the family group and were dominant.

Both herding and farming existed alongside one another and each of them, regularly, supplied the needs of the other. Both produced surpluses sufficient for trading for the other's surplus and gained by it. However, by and large, the farmers were less dependent on the herders' provisions than conversely. During the earlier millennia of farming along river valleys of the Middle East, peasant kingdoms had the upper hand (Eph'al, 1982).

Later on, however, herders became dominant thanks to forging a strategic force and the ability to move between the two communities. The peasant workforce was and remained the family group, which did not encourage unions. Shepherding on the other hand was and remained the responsibility of a group. Society's main objective has been a lasting need felt by people to stand together and help one another vis-à-vis the outside. Tribal unification enabled Bedouin cohorts to prevail in battle against numerically larger groups. Moving with their property, their herds, nomadic people could present greater fighting units, allowing them to overcome sedentary communities one after the other and thereby cause havoc and deter potential foes from fighting back.

The many men a tribe could recruit in times of danger and mobilize them all to battle, the better were its chances of success and the more secure its members could feel. Joining forces was crucial to obtaining common objectives where stratification is based on large groups at the top. Individual objectives were attainable through union. Each tribesman was brought up to know that behind him stands the political might of his tribe. A massive combat camp was needed to fight other tribes and centers of sedentary population. Men who were loyal to one another were sustained in this union. A social infrastructure made up of tribes obligated the retention of organizations based on warriors' cohorts of men trained to preserve the tribal code of behavior. Tribal existence and varied ascriptions were at the base of upbringing throughout this Culture Area. Although men are born individuals, tribe members received encouragement to keep the tribe going, to assure the appearance of every possible man in times of emergency, to join forces.

Men were called to advance matters of honor and mutual material interest. This could be over pastureland, matters of *manashed,* i.e., judgments related to women's honor and, no less significant, personal status and honor (Kressel & Bar Zvi, 1991). Reasons to fight do appear, and even if they do not occur frequently they are part of a lasting intra-tribal reality. This means that each of them would abandon his economic activities in favor of matters that regard their tribe as a whole. To leave one's herd behind for a while in order to help the tribe settle its inter-tribal affairs before returning to personal business means to place matters of social politics first, over individual economic concerns.

Along with the normative tribal code, first it is essential to have individual concerns accord with the common cause. Submitting to their common cause is necessary since acting within the social universe of tribes leaves no other way out. Harmonizing a joint action obligates the group because it preconditions its success. A climate of political obedience to elders (Sheikhs) signifies accountability to the tribal cause, i.e., disregard for personal concerns when the public interest calls. The division of obligations is often narrow; a tribesman tends his private property (livestock) alone, but guarding the safety of herds is the function and duty of his allies, his tribesmen.

Protecting herds against thieves and pastureland against intrusion by rival groups obliges them to cooperate and act as a disciplined unit, a political one. This protection requires that the tribe members follow a single voice of command. Solidarity places them in the immediate social environment as a combatant unity. When the emblem of unity is the tribe's founding forefathers the meaning is an order according to which cohorts of people are referred to as the semen of an individual who lived generations earlier and implies the willingness to risk one's life defending the group's concerns. A prime political concern among tribes is their relative size that determines their status. The prime concern shared by them all is standing together vis-à-vis others. Patrilineal tribes form a political entity, not necessarily an economic one. Continuity of the tribe's existence implies maintaining the combatant unity. Groups of men are judged by their size that is conventionally approved loyalty to a common political cause. Tribesmen are expected to appear on time once called to arms, when a quarrel occurs, either between two of their group mates or a rival, who is "Other," in this sense, a member of another tribe.

Power structure in a traditional Middle Eastern society is based on the relative size of agnatic groups, the principal determinant of group status. Of course, groups of agnates can inflate the size of their cohorts, since no accurate census is kept and many relatives live outside the tribes' immediate neighborhood.

A common front depends on fulfilling the obligation facing the members to abandon all private concerns and avail themselves as combatants, aiding the tribe to overcome a dispute over pastureland or a blood feud successfully, thus attaining its bit of political objective.

Elders muster their men called to fight together. They are on guard to defend joint interests and not least matters of honor when challenged. A tribesman who is called to take up his sword and die for a tribal cause cannot slip away and retain a general concern for his individual interests once he has stood at the front, challenged by others.

Tribesmen are referred to as progeny of a founding father, children of the same father, not necessarily of the same mother. They are descendants of one forefather, whose name is recalled and used in order to include the tribal ancestor who lived generations earlier. At the same time they could be descendents of different grandmothers, as in fact were the biblical Jacob's (= Israel) forebearers, mothers of the Twelve Tribes. The father matters most in accordance with this social norm and practice, which has fundamentally been retained in the social array of the Middle East ever since. The offspring are largely named after him or called jointly his sons, who share, by being from his semen, "one blood."

In accordance with this standard, conventionally, the tribe's status is ranked by estimation of the maximal number of sword holders it can mobilize. Cohorts of pastoralists are relatively easier to mobilize, as compared to farmers, because their property, their herds, can be moved along with them. Bedouin, fewer in number, were able to occupy vast lands, densely populated with peasants and townspeople. The 7th century tribesmen streaming from Arabia conquered the Middle East; Huns, Mongols and Turks, streaming from central Asia westward, overwhelmed Europe and the Middle East. Upon settling down and changing their occupations, the tribal framework has been preserved as long as it could be, though with less success in Europe.

Prior to the use of firearms, the tribal bond committed men to fight shoulder to shoulder, thereby improving their position up the social pyramid. Sticks and sword fights required outnumbering their rivals on the battlefield. Every armed man was needed to secure success. An offence aiming to better the tribe's status or a defensive fight in answer to challengers protected the tribe's status which was their common objective.

A joint status of tribesmen vis-à-vis their allies and foes was a function of ascription that always came before personal achievement. As long as the group did not face any danger it could allow its men to spread out over large areas, provided of course that they paid attention to any call to appear and join their group's fighters when they were needed. The greater one's forces were the higher their success rate and their position on the social ladder. Lower in the hierarchy were tribes of smaller numbers of men. Once the greater the number of fighters meant forsaking one's family and material interests at home — to stand by the tribe in battle, to risk life on being called to the fight, was highly respected. Manhood was counted and tested through various trials.

Adherence with one's tribal core and sacrifice in an effort to retain the tribe's esteem is a crucial test. Closely related to their joint status vis-à-vis others are neighboring groups. Polygyny and maximization of reproduction indicate a lasting race for social status.

Of late, in several Middle Eastern States, conflict among Sheikhs and of heads of minority groups has increased. While losing power, weakening Nation States stop providing the civil services expected from them, and this has compelled citizens to attain what they are missing independently. Masses of people who have learned then for some sixty years to rely on civil services have been obliged to rely on themselves, thus reverting to ways they had in the past.

Since 2011, over the last years, some Nation States in the Middle East have regressed to experience a social realism in which they lived in years prior to the becoming states. Where central governments have lost control on both foreign and domestic affairs, most of the services offered by them to their citizens have stopped abruptly. While the State organs are reaching a condition of paralysis and failure to operate, i.e., to provide civil services, citizens begin to rely upon their backbone of agnates.

Relatedness to paternal relatives is largely reinforced lest they may be called to be used politically. Out of the tribal regime comes the infrastructure that remains the extended family group and the tribe, the most primal and long lasting for all eventualities. These frameworks supplement for the deficiencies of State authorities.

Once intra-tribal affairs come to dominate society, matters of agnatic ascription attain precedence over all other commitments that people may have. In addition, preoccupation with tribal affairs diminishes the role of national concerns in peoples' minds. Seizure of power by Sheikhs may spread to include State positions such as those that enable them to meddle in rival tribes' concerns or matters of honor, which are of utmost important.

Along with the *salafi* movement that encourages volunteers to fight the "infidel," that include believers of other creeds, developed the desire to square accounts with domestic rivals, thus intra-*Umma* wars began. Unconventional use of power, once it occurs, escalates abuses of arms, all the more so in the present-day states with no effective government. Positions abandoned by modern Middle East governments, accentuate an infrastructure where it has remained tribal. The use of firearms may alter traditional conceptions of warrior numbers. Small, well armed, organized tribes can overcome their larger rival cohorts. Non-conventional use of arms expedites the annulment of State laws.

Nonfunctioning of a civil service can last for years and in as much as a **massive power** is the rule of the political game it puts aside expectations for a system's improvement. When the single key for reshuffling office holders is another tribe that can take hold of the power of the State, the citizens desire the success of another tribe. There is no individual way out of a bureaucratic predicament save for the triumph of another tribe. Decreased holding of State positions does not invite resentment directed to the system as a whole or to bureaucracy in general, but, rather for a strong hand to appear and strike order again.

In as long as ascription and tribal identity decide upon appointment of office holders, and objective qualifications needed to carry out these offices comes second, a desire for bettering the service means reshuffling of the ruling tribe. Objective perceptions of protected positions are hard to limit in a tribal regime. Recruitment of mayors of villages, of towns and of States remains an intertribal affair and clashes over positions are unavoidable. Tribes that succeed in a power struggle try their best to rest on their laurels, to consider further effort to be unnecessary, i.e., reinforce their hold over possessions and retain power as long as they can.

Functions that were forsaken by the vanishing State organs in several Mid Eastern countries (like Libya) over the last four years have not been taken over by others and remain vacant. The trouble in a lack of office succession is not a matter of convention or discontent over the rules of this game but in a lack of sufficiently strong combatant tribes to come and capture the vacant positions.

Repressed memory of *salafi* disagreements in the world of Islam have been reawakened in the last few years. Remembering these historic events and the old disputes renewed argumentation and then enmity and, soon after, exchange of fire. Facing the future could provide reform of old formulae and the acceptance of the eternal that is in this creed, and limit restraint.

41

Salafi enmities have been rekindled upon discovering their ancient accounts and soon after a return to exchange of fire across street barriers. Recollection of events as regards the first century of Islam brings to the fore memories pertaining to the Shi'ah–Sunna rift that makes the ancient enmity relevant and lasting. The present wars in the region are nourished by recollection of events and enmity that evolved some fourteen centuries ago. The region's society then and now is comprised of tribes and ethnic minorities.

Having no superstructure and agreed-upon authority above them all, rival tribes find themselves at war with one another. Where State organs fail to control their people in peace and alternative offices to fulfill these functions are out of reach, public order crumbles. Rules needed to govern fail to rebuild inter-tribal cooperation, allowing dissension to reign.

The spread of sectarian feuds focuses attention on the infrastructure or on the way neighboring societies are comprised. The similarity of tribal units accompanies the desire for self-sufficiency. The tendency to limit exchange between tribes hinders "organic solidarity" (Durkheim, 1893). Because urban areas are independent means there is no exchange of any kind. Interdependence comes with professional specification, a quality that facilitates the growth of peace.

Enmity grows more frequent where town quarters are subdivided in accordance with agnatic ascription, when self-sufficient groups reject unification. Exchange of fire across street barriers is then a constant threat. Durkheim taught us the divide between "organic solidarity" due to the division of labor and "mechanical solidarity" through likeness. Tribal likeness is the trouble that the introduction of Islam came to solve. *Umma* is perceived as a shadow term, like an "umbrella," which was opened in order to include all tribes under it. A search for an ideal common denominator that would contain all believers of Sunni Islam regardless of their ethnic ascription is endorsed anew by groups active in the area of eastern Syria and western Iraq.

Allah's sayings are often impervious or disguised; his words are suggestive or hinting though rarely emphatic and even if colloquial, they do not resemble the way people speak. Allah does not embellish his sayings and if he sounds vague, he does not do it to embarrass the dreamer. Elements that make the message difficult to interpret are a result of God's thoughts that often require effort to interpret. Nevertheless Allah's sayings rarely remain opaque. If unfamiliar to the dreamer or misunderstood, some people specialize in "opening dreams." Traditional interpreters use a number of methods to draw sense out of rude dream material. One of those is by means of a coffee cup test.

Dreamers search for clues in dreams, all the more so when at a crossroads or when the group awaits a message of what to do or where to go, when all look forward, expecting instructions "from above." Dreams that touch on private matters are let alone, that is, left to remain personal or unnoticed by the dreamers' agnates.

I. Matters of Theoretical Concern

Dreams Told in Public

Of the early anthropological interest given to the public importance of dreams in society I learned from the work of A.F.C. Wallace (1958). His essay deals with early studies of reference to dreams among the Tsonnontouen (Seneca) Indians of North America, beginning at the 17th century. Prevalent among the tribes was the belief in a single soul that animates the human body and gives it life, knowledge, desire, judgment and a capacity to leave the body during dreams and after death. The soul occupied all parts of the human anatomy as an ethereal counterpart to the physical body.

Aspirations of the soul belonging to the person seen in a dream, be it one who is still alive or one who is long dead, must be respected with awe. Due respect to souls in dreams is not a matter of courtesy as much as it is a fear of God and of punishment from Heaven. From high above, the souls sent into our dreams look upon our living or dead counterparts. Truthful regard for their demands is therefore no less obligating. We dreamers are required to recall the dream's message and listen carefully when it invites us to action [235].

The Iroquoian people let dreams redirect their lives [236]. Particulars of their reference to dreams reached the knowledge of C.G. Jung and S. Freud. Familiarity with the Iroquois theory of dreams strengthened both their belief in the psychic unity of mankind and for theories of "primitive" thought where things happened, that element of secret desires of the soul revolting against the body, causing diseases and even death. "*Ondinnonk*" is a secret desire of the soul manifested by a dream that obligates the dreamer to fulfill it. The difficulty occurs when the manifest contents of dreams are either held back or concealed, thus not showing the soul's true desire to the dreamer.

Unsophisticated acceptance of the dreams' meaning does not distinguish conscious from unconscious parts of mind. Thus the supernatural vision needs to see into the depths of soul's requests. Some people in every society apparently develop the ability to fulfill this position.

Experienced analysts may have the ability to read dreams connected with a capacity to interpret deceased persons' appearance in dreams and speculate as to what they are saying. When ghosts speak or their words are animated, thus providing a pronouncement through a dream, they can play a renewing role in the life of dreamers that include their group of agnates. Dreams in which the tribe's elders (forefathers) appear frequently occur at a time of stress due to domestic disputes. Elders are expected to appear in dreams when intra-tribal disputes occur or are about to happen, provoking potential conflicts, when the voice of the Divine is expected to raise the group's spirits, when a command from above, from Allah's court, seems to be needed to encourage. At times warning dreams appear unexpectedly and thus are understood as foretelling a possible domestic dispute that may evolve and spoil the order. Concern for preserving harmony cannot be taught or embraced on an individual's whim or a reflection of his own fortuitous desires. Nor is it a reflection of a dreamer's whim. It is broadly viewed as a warning sign sent down from heaven to afford the one approached the choice of salvation, conditioned on piety: Saving one's life depends on fearing Allah.

A Person's Dream and a Warning for All

Former Bedouin now living in town, among whom I spent several years of anthropological fieldwork,[14] took dreams in which their ancestors appeared as a serious call requiring their attention and cohesion. Details of encounters with elders in dreams are brought to the knowledge of everybody concerned. On the whole, when they were brought to my attention as well, I found such dreams, that they understood to be directed from Allah, to mean a call for greater tribal unity. Viewed as arriving from the depths of the grave and/or from God's court in heaven, cases in which an elder has been seen in a dream are of necessity a matter of family concern.

Rumors of a family member who happened to see an old Sheikh in a dream thus motivates listeners to hear about it from him openly, to tell his (rarely also her) dream to his agnates, his closest agnates, who deserve more and are obliged to receive more than other extended paternal family members.

Other kinds of dreams, of whatever intimate content, rarely reach the knowledge of others to thus be a part of a public concern. Why is it that long deceased tribal elders, who are remembered in tales only, seem to be longed for? Along with my fieldwork, listening to individuals telling of a forefather they dreamed about, I marked parenthetically in my notebook as indicating a rising problem of group cohesion.

Old photographs of parents and grandparents frequently decorate walls of homes and their re-appearance is understandable and largely taken as a call to quiet disputants.

---

[14] Anthropological fieldwork beginning in late 1967 until 1969 proceeded on and off during the 1970s and with visits and retaining contacts and hosting of community members until the present day.

They appear thereby to urge their descendents to come to terms, arrive at a compromise (to forestall the evil of a dispute in sight) to maintain the group's unity.

Beseeching unity and dreams to boost the acting together typify times of pressure, whether arising from within (at times of domestic disputes) or caused by a challenging outsider. The appearance of elders in dreams is largely taken as a warning that is an indication of trouble, indicative of a social problem. The wellbeing of a tribe's spirit comes to be tested at moments of need, when incorporation is in question, urging all to forget alleged reasons for domestic strife and to join forces. Domestic hostility to the extent of intra-family squabbles spoils the solidarity needed to prepare for a battle, confront external rivals which consequently threatens the unity needed vis-à-vis hostile others. In order to get ready for a time when the real objective is loyalty to agnates in combat solidarity is a must.

Once Ascription is Cut on Principles of Agnation

Agnates are individuals related to one another as kin by virtue of a patri-lateral grandfather, i.e., present-day people who are committed to one another politically by virtue of them all being descendents of a common male ancestor, an individual forefather who lived generations ago. Naturally, the longer the span of generations since this person's lifetime, the greater is the potential number of combatant individuals for whom his name is the flag. Recollection of a ramified genealogical tree is beyond the ability of most everyone, particularly the illiterate among them. However, the few Sheikhs who specialize and are trained and know it by heart can serve the tribe to inculcate these facts to the younger people, at temporal occasions when the tribe's warriors get together.

Including maternal kin alongside the paternal ones, i.e., **cognates** and also **affine** relatives, may provide a larger group when needed, to stand together vis-à-vis challenging others. However, increasing the circle of supporters, the group category that sets together individuals who are expected to stretch a helping hand to one another in time of trouble, by virtue of being relatives, can double their number. Descendents of an ancient pair of mother and father, like Abraham and Hagar, who are the ultimate grandparents of all descending ages, lead to the present day neighboring tribes and Middle Eastern nations.

Ancient conceptions of ascription still hold true to minimize the biological and social importance of traits inherited through mothers. Accentuation of one's belonging to one's *'umûm* on the account of one's *ikhwâl* defines contemporary people as tribes by virtue of their common forefathers, who may be persons who lived generations ago. This social setup that differs compared to all embracing consanguine ascription profoundly impacts the psychology of the people engaged.

Allocation of equal importance to cognates broadens the circle of mutual expectations for help when needed. Co-dependence for economic and political support, once required, encouraged widening circles of potential support, viz., maximizing the number of people at one's service, for any emergency. Acknowledging all consanguine people as relatives doubles the circle of support when in need to enlarge the belt of security. The potential source of help grows still bigger once one's affinity circle is included too, which maximizes the circle of relatives. However, the rules founded on patrilineal principals diminish the weight of possible support stemming from "foreign" sources. A helping hand when in need is welcome from wherever it comes, so it would be, e.g., in face of natural disasters. Then all relatives count. The fact of being related to one another as agnates, i.e., being the progeny of a great grandfather, a common ancestor is a reflection of a lasting need, felt by them, many men jointly, to be united and ready for action, to ward off **political** attacks.

Present-day tribesmen who remain allies *ad hoc* and potential comrades-in-arms, now as townsmen, as they ever were,[15] are brought up committed to stand by and support one another. Once extended families, lineages and tribes, predominate the social scene, adherence to one's own group of agnates remains powerful, and results in being their second nature. Inculcation of readiness to be called for help then fight jointly by the side of a relative (by definition a paternal one) when at risk, signifies as a rule *'umûm* only, i.e., those belonging to one's father's line of descent, which precludes dying for *ikhwâl*, who are one's consanguine relatives through the mother.

Striving for a better position up the social ladder means engaging in fights with most neighboring lineages of approximately equal numbers of combatant men. Once mobility up the social ladder exposes lineages to feuding relationships, susceptibility to colliding with one another is apparent; feuding relationships can last until one of them tips the scale in its favor. In a social milieu where the extent of lineages provides their position on the status ladder, paternal kin groups need to make every effort to retain their unity.

Closing all possible gaps between their combatant kin becomes fundamental to achieve victory. Paternal lineages are prone to clash on matters of honor with those who are nearly equal to them in size. Any pretext to answer claims of offence with blows may result in interpersonal problems. While the conflict is between a large versus a small group, words and compensation fees can resolve issues. A situation of conflict occurs where palliative words do not assuage the rival tribes

---

[15] See Kressel, G.M. (1996). *Ascendancy Through Aggression.*

or lineage groups. Causes of friction leading to blows are often of a kind of inter-tribal issue, not domestic conditions or civil problems in nature, or a matter of class struggle or of belief or creed, but rather — the relative size and the status accorded to their numerical position. The apparently equal in size are therefore susceptible to grave struggles about status.

Associations of a patrilineal order bind family members together as kin by virtue of being descendents of one male ancestor. The richer the depth of recollection, i.e., the genealogical knowledge, the greater is the present-day combatant group of agnates. Genealogical trees therefore shape the relative size of combatant units of men to be mobilized on occasion for fighting alongside one another against others, when in need.

This current system follows the old tradition current in Europe, Africa and Asia, long prevailing, historically known from the ancient Middle East and from ancient Rome. Political relatedness of men, descendents of a great grandfather, forms the winning political union, unless they do not stand with one another. The tribal effort to attain hegemony and, upon achieving it, to retain it for as long as possible calls on its men to unite. It spurs reproduction and keeps the corporation of agnates intact, pending the hour of need, lest it may soon appear and find them not on speaking terms, i.e., once the tribe is not healthily united.

Dreams and an Objective Truth

An appearance of one's grandparents in dreams is natural all the more so when they take or took an intensive part in their offspring's life. Mother's mother and father's mother not less than father's father and mother's father are seen in dreams equally frequently. But father's father or his father's father and even more distant persons like a legendary great grandfather who no one recalls since he lived generations ago and hence is recalled by name only — once he appears in a dream, can cause excitement among his male offspring. Great grandpa's contact with his posterity, skipping over generations, is imaginary and thought of as a symbol of importance that is inculcated to be of general importance.

In some traditional societies (see Stanner, 1956), the dreams that appear to individuals provide a kind of narrative of things that once happened; a kind of charter of things that still happen; and a kind of logos or principle of order transcending all that is significant in life for the entire group.

Particular kinds of night dreams are searched for and once they occur to an individual, his group mates signify the dream as an event and a message that reached them from afar, carrying an important warning for the group as a whole. Among former Bedouin now living in town, who I happened to know and work with, one's paternal kin, mostly male elders (i.e., agnates), are one's circle or forum that counts as the innermost group of kin. Tribal ascription endures after half a century of living in town. At the same time, encounters in a dream with a person (usually only one in a dream),[16] belonging to this group's elders, once occurred, is taken as a pronouncement for the attention of the group's living elders. The event is therefore related to others who are requested to become aware of it. It happens that the content of dreams is brought to the attention of still more people who have some memory of the person although they do not refer to him in practice.

Still remembered elders, who passed away not long ago, or ones who lived generations ago, are expected to appear in dreams and relate things of importance to their progeny. In this social

---

[16] Following my listening to dream stories, rarely do several elders appear in one and the same dream.

environment "archetypal" dreams are largely considered if revealed in them are bearded men, viz. great grandfathers. The mother archetype and the great grandmothers once appearing in dreams, as studied by Jung, call for a look at counterbalancing traits that show in archetypal dreams in which great grandfathers appear. Expecting the appearance in dream of a Sheikh in the capacity of a sage, radiating an aura of traditional wisdom who comes to see his grandchildren, is a primary expectation among former Negev Bedouin now living in the town of Ramle.

Different cultural climates may in fact accentuate the frequency of paternal (rather than maternal) archetypes in dreams. Here images of instructive Sheikhs predominate the dreamers' desire. While the mother archetype is marked by traits like "goodness, passion and darkness,"[17] the father archetype as imparted in dreams is largely a person who looks out for his progeny's fate and does it wisely, bravely and wholeheartedly loving, not selfishly, never avenging, passionate or looking backward in rage. He stands as ever as an emblem in his offspring's mind, filling the position of their joint (tribal) conscience and concerns, to preserve their united strength, sufficient for the promise that they might overcome obstacles to secure their survival.

Once dreams of supplication occur they are recognized as carrying a message from the Divine to the living, be it to warn the agnate group or to get their attention anew to retain their unity, to stand together facing their fate, prepare jointly to meet their imminent future.[18]

---

[17] Jung ([1959] 1972). The Mother Archetype, the Mother-Complex: Positive Aspects of the Mother Complex. *Four Archetypes; Mother, Rebirth, Spirit, Trickster,* pp. 15- 44.

[18] For a renewed attempt to sum up the organizational demands favored by herder societies and their related view of the divine, see Meeker (1989), *The Pastoral Son.*

Uncovering messages out of their concealed dream veil calls for training or basic experience with psychoanalysis. It means removal of less important details that decorate dreams and remaining with a simple, palpable message. Once hidden, divine messages appear it is crucial for the group's survival to decipher and take heed of what they are. Why God favors this method of transferring his directions for tribes' consideration is a secret. Often the message in dreams needs sifting before it makes sense. The abundance of features can obscure sight and many of them, once removed, make it more distinct. A convoluted garb may color the dream's appearance and need be "pulled out" before it makes sense. Once "undressed" dreams make sense that they did not before and the question is, how better to establish the story's true meaning? Why not present it simply, with no adornment at all? What is the fancy decoration and why dress it like a riddle?

Discussions concerning the value of dream material often arouse the questions and commonly provide the answers too, saying that whatever it is in regards to the lineage is the substance, i.e., matters of merely individual concern do not merit talking about. Given that the dreams we have come from Allah, then why does it come mixed, putting the important with the irrelevant things together? And why does it [the dream] try us, making us guess which part of it is the important one?

To accentuate our tribe's concerns, simply, is of prime importance. It is not a riddle or a game played with us when we accept this basic rule. Viewing dreams as if they were sent from the Divine (from Heaven) important dreams are those to be told to the group, to help one's kin know right from wrong. Dreams that recommend or reprimand certain kinds of behavior do so with a view of group objectives of coping with future challenges.

Visions signaling the correct path for one's tribe to take are often an expression of personal desire. At times I noticed that individuals who had missed a moment of glory hoped through dreams to return to the group's heart and hence to be respected by it. In striving to regain the attention of group mates, the appearance that Allah had provided the impetus would be beyond doubt the best. Personal communion with supernatural powers may occur to youngsters and elders, women and men alike, although middle-aged men seem more susceptible to be addressed; in fact they are heard in public more than others.

Once men have a proper dream to tell most likely I thought they would find a way to relate it, perhaps first privately and then in public. I learned that visions are expected or sought by all; youngsters, also girls, may surprise their elders with claims of having had visions. A visionary encounter with a great grandfather is rightly "archetypal" and not less frequent than (per C. G. Jung[19]) a *nomina* of a great grandmother. A great grandfather, or the psychological image of his lasting presence, counts more than any other societal representation for his descendents, wherever they live.

The tribal fabric in urban quarters retains its hold and as of late, in some of the region's countries, appears coherent to external observers too. Civil wars, wherever they occur, tear away the civil aspect of the town's quarters to exhibit the reality of tribal subdivisions. More than divisions by social classes or trade zones residents' neighborhoods differ by tribal ascription. Largely speaking, the region's town quarters resemble one another by virtue of being "tribal." Lineages counting many hundreds of individuals live alongside one another, whether rich or poor.

---

[19] For further definitions see C. G. Jung (1964 [1959]). *Four Archetypes*, p. 10.

The names of founding Sheikhs designate the tribal subdivisions, the intra-structure in suburbs of towns. Long deceased fathers who are believed to guard their descendents from the other world are expected to appear and show needed guidelines. Unclear moments in life and the yearning to be lead by the Divine then lead to openness, giving meaning to dreams. Messages carried by dreams are then taken as pronouncements, as heralds arriving from a mysterious realm to tell the group, e.g., of imminent danger, pertaining to their joint fate and showing them the safe way to proceed. Hence dreams are like calls from afar, foretelling threatening events and offering ways to forestall danger.

On recognizing a dream message, its timing is a part of the puzzle: Why was it sent to us precisely now, in the form of a dream to A or B? Weighing those as calls from heaven the significance of dreams is a joint concern, acknowledged by all. At times of particular constraints when questions of survival arise, councils are necessary. They are then dealt with socially, compelling everyone to seek a solution.

Dreams containing cultural symbolism are passively expected and gratefully welcomed. As well, certain dream sights can be actively sought after, and once they occur, they are taken as a divine response, answering the human plea. Once agnatic dreams occur they are announced and brought to the general awareness. The group considers a sight observed in one person's dream as part of everyone's concern.

Other kinds of dreams may be considered as "unsought," to be left "unnoticed." Another category of visions or dream sights is referred to as revolting and therefore not worth attention or pronouncement. In fact, foretelling dreams are traditionally known and therefore they are awaited. On being expected, to an extent, such dreams are identified beforehand.

II. Ponder the Topic
of Dreams

Talk of Dreams Along with Anthropological Fieldwork

Along with anthropological fieldwork (1966-1972) among former Bedouin now living in Ramle,[20] in two of the town's quarters I attended occasions of dream telling sometimes at small group get-togethers, both in homes and in the neighborhood *shiq*.[21] Dreams were also related to me in private, people stopping me while I was walking in the street or visiting in people's homes. Having been attentive to personal concerns not less than to socio-cultural ones (e.g., Kressel, 1977; 1980)[22] brought people, occasionally, to tell me or ask me about dreams they had had. My presence and patient listening summoned appeals, largely of men but often of women, too, to ask for my opinion as regards dreams or repeated dream imagery that occurred to them.

---

[20] A mixed Arab-Jewish town some 60 kilometers southeast of Tel Aviv.

[21] The Council of Elders in town: A shack or hut, under eucalyptus trees, on a small hill where the group elders get together, a few of them from morning on and several more after work, in the evening.

[22] Bride Price Reconsidered. *Current Anthropology* 1977; 18 (3): 441-458. Agnatic Endogamy as a Cultural Mode of Social Stratification: FBD & FBS Marriage in Jawarish. *Asian and African Studies* 1980; 14(3): 255-268.

Being mainly concerned with community study, lineage setting and tribal affairs, as an anthropologist I was not preoccupied with psychological concerns. Hence, on being approached to decipher dreams, I used to make my professional expertise (which was not psychology) clear, but, nevertheless, people who habitually talked with me felt free to approach me, eager to hear what I could add about their dreams.

Some acquaintance with the art of dream analysis and with writings of S. Freud (1933) and C.G. Jung (1953-1979) had made me attentive to dreams. People who approached me during my anthropological fieldwork, and some did afterwards as well,[23] wishing to hear what I could say on that which they saw while asleep, had largely found me attentive, never bored. Since I was patient, listening to details of the images described and discussed and asking for minor details when missing, individuals called me in days afterwards to fill in gaps I was interested in. It occurred to me to take note of what I heard.

When I contemplated my field notes while writing my dissertation I codified the mention of dreams but did not use this material due to the different emphasis of study. Leaving it for a more suitable future time, the years went by. In 2010, I searched through my old notes for those stories of dreams, about which people once had told me. I now gave more thought to frequent, repeating elements of dream stories that had elucidated cases of agnation. Repetition of stories of old Sheikhs seen and also heard in a dream gave me the impression of an expected kind of vision that duly came true; a wished for an event that provided the dreamer a stage; he was asked for more details and the answers were discussed by all. If not expected by all, at least I thought it suited persons placed (relatively) in social obscurity. Expecting to be listened to and

---

[23] Until 1978, I lived nearby and since then, over the years I moved on, living in the Negev.

addressed by all can be adesirable position. Telling and hearing the details of visions are vital because these facts of life can be shown by the Almighty to one's agnates. Dreams as such are a common concern for agnate groups, the forum obligating some political unity.

The frequency of elder Sheikhs appearing in dreams, I assume, is not necessarily different than the appearance of grandmothers in dreams, but the meaning of and preparation for grandfathers' in dreams are greater. In other words, the expectancy for Sheikhs' dreams proved overt and once they occur they were received with greater attention, all the more so among descendents, i.e., the paternal progeny of the Sheikhs concerned.[24]

During these years, in view of the dreams that were brought to my attention, I thought of them mainly as messages addressed from the unconscious, to alter the dreamers' position in their social setting. Pointing at mental predicaments of dreamers indicating that each one's unconscious presses us back into balance produced little comment from me although I pondered it much. For me then listening meant showing concern and attention to supplicants in the community I studied and to their problems. It had occurred to me that I felt I had to think and read more before I could return to a supplicant. Often, to elaborate on a bizarre presentation of a dream I felt I had to read more or to consult a person who knew more, who belonged to the psychoanalytic profession.

My answers to questions asking for explanations of dreams included a reference to symbols. Whatever I could add about

---

[24] For a succinct analysis of the "spirit of patriarchy" as it is related to herding societies, see Meeker (1989), *The Pastoral Son*, pp. 60-66. Among East African herding societies the position and authority of fathers and elders along with the clan divinities, together with agnatic principals, are promoted.

our unconscious choice of people dreamed about, "why just those and not others," I explained that those are the people we think about but not enough; or too much for no good reason; those for whom we sense needlessly worry, love or anger, etc. Often people dreamed about come to request a change in reference. Much depends on what they mean for us, or the contrary of our expectations to get from them. One's actual position vis-à-vis a person dreamed about brings to mind a suggestion to reconsider our attitude towards her/him and a change of manners, be it encouragement to greater trust or the opposite.

On following the mention of dreams spread through my field notes of some forty years earlier, I come to notice in them deducible traits of which I had not been aware. At that time I referred to each dream description only with its personal, concrete background, and on looking at it again, in these last years, an overview allowed me see in them connecting and repetitious qualities. The general patterns in which Sheikhs appear followed an old-fashion prototype. Somewhere in my text I added the words that Sheikhs are expected to return the way the Messiah is awaited among the Jews.

Comparing prototypes of an elder Sheikh appearing in dreams evinced a basic similarity, which as a common denominator is answerable to a cultural pattern. Worship of forefathers is therefore shared at this culture area.

Terms of Reference, Patrilineal Descent Groups and Agnation

The principal of agnation is broadly phrased as follows: a system of measuring kinship only through the male members of a family. It was used in ancient Rome and it is still practiced throughout the Middle East. "Agnatic" pertains to the reckoning of relationship by male links exclusively, regardless of sex of Ego and/or Alter. An agnate, then, is a person related by patrilineal descent. In Roman law *"agnati"* were kin who traced their relationship by descent through males only, from a common ancestor, who were under the authority of a single paterfamilias, and who resided together. Agnation included women, but no kin linked through a woman. Although agnates were "uterine" kin, the connection to a common mother was obliterated and hardly ever mentioned in talks.

An anthropological search for the extended influence of the agnatic principal, reaching beyond the immediate family group, reveals the prevalent array of tribes. In deserts as well as in urban settings of the Middle East, the social infrastructure is drawn heavily on the viewpoint of manhood. Idealization of virility limits men's behavior by suppressing inclinations, also found among men, to imitate feminine behavior. This essence in turn wrought the region's culture and its social norms.

Radical segregation of the two "gender camps" in all public arenas and to an extent also in homes accentuates a divided mode of being with regards to traits shared by all humans alike. Human modes of behavior that are shared despite gender are thus overlooked to segregate individuals into two gendered categories. Gendered methods in child upbringing shape two distinct ways of behavior in successive generations over millennia. Rigid gender distinctions set social activities and social rules and prevail over the entire extent of human activity. Natural stability depends on these behavioral traditions based on ways of thinking.

Resistance to change implies a broad "disregard" of the (Western) world's pace of liberation, relaxing the ancient gender divisions. Nowhere in the cultural arena of Middle Eastern Bedouin do gender distinctions capitulate to become egalitarian and to the prevalence of modern ways. Here, the idea of the free encounter of the sexes, in all public spheres, is largely rejected. Gender distinctions shape alike women's and men's view of the self and of the other, and society at large, regardless of generation and of age distinctions, embraces this.

Similar traits of importance that most of my (former Bedouin) correspondents shared on discussing dreams assumed the predominant male elders rule that commits them as tribesmen. Expectation to meet and receive a whispered pronouncement of wisdom by a forefather ("*jîd—jîd—jîdy*" = father of father of my father - -) in a night dream was therefore considered an event of prime importance.

Despite all readjustments required upon moving from the desert to living in modern towns and the radical change concomitant with the new way of living, the tribal settling does not temper its hold. Contacts among members are now run via cellular phones, but there is no replacement to alter contemporary people's sense of tradition. They continue to rely on the enduring patripotestal[25] tradition.

Analytical Guidelines

Maintaining a modern way of urban life has engaged the younger generation of Bedouin living in town in a renewed awareness of the social security they are losing. Had it come in yearned for or sought after figures of white bearded forefathers in dreams to reassure the dreamer of the new life one maintains in town? Or had it arrived as a warning against succumbing to thoughtless desires, to a too far reaching transition, away from the elders' consensus as individuals distancing themselves from the group's norms? Here elders assemble in their neighborhood

---

[25] Referring to the enduring exercise of authority by a paternal great grandfather.

shiq to discuss domestic and countrywide political affairs; here they listen to the "*shiq* spirit" or "judgment" and say what they think about it.

One way or another, when forefathers were summoned in dreams, for me it signified a change of emphasis, to return to an ancient social order. Such dreams reflect an inner call to live on better terms with one's forefathers' tradition, which means in the first instance to sharpen one's recollection, to recall what it was, to embrace the *salafi*,[26] the legendary, and uphold tradition, maintain it faithfully, day by day. To pull the distant past closer indicates revitalizing awareness of the ancient comportment — the way it presented itself to one's predecessors.

Idealization of the way one's forefathers lived implies an ideal form of life to be followed, change away from a day-to-day way of living on the track of modernity. Behavior that adheres to that of one's ancestor generations may be conceived as a way that promises rewards in this world or a promise for rewards in the world beyond. To behave in the light of the past means to an extent a negation of modernity, of current patterns of conduct of private and of social affairs.

A sought after kind of dream can be equated with finding a treasure; it is a culturally acquired desire, which comes "from above" to confirm the presence of providence, of the Divine. Joint expectations, shared by a group, are not necessarily the outcome of formal inculcation. It becomes a desire by attention to oral traditions, stories of elders who were brought up to know things by listening to elders, etc. Dreams may be thought of as signs of the Divine that lead us to a goal; a heavenly means to

---

[26] *Salafi* = predecessor, ancestor. The *salafi* age account for the age of Muhammad Abdalla, the Prophet of Islam.

correct the course of events that should guide the group and lead it to fulfill God's plan for it.[27]

As a command that comes "from above," the dream better directs one's fate on condition that this dream would improve behavior and hence please the Almighty. Tribesmen yield to their tribe's requirements over their private ones. To please one's group counts more than the satisfaction of any personal need. Sought out dreams seem to be colored by norms signaling the priority of their social mission. Their moral code and their joint, interpersonal objectives match the tribal interests.

Through the ages, elders in charge of the group's survival are therefore beseeched to better conduct tribal affairs and strengthen the tribe's longevity to enhance the common interest. Among descendents of desert Bedouin ideal dreams were those where a forefather appeared to differentiate right from wrong for the dreamer. As a rule, there is no mention here of conscious attitudes that may nourish or color unconscious revelations. Dreams that transmit views of paternal forefathers, who symbolize the tribe's unity, are received as calls from afar, calling their descendents to strike a domestic unity and together prepare for challenging events.

Unlike the commotion surrounding the Oedipal Complex, focusing on parents-offspring, mother-son and father-daughter

---

[27] "Dreams are the royal road to the ancestors. The ancestral spirits, venerated in the indigenous religion are believed to use the dream as their chief means of communication with this world. In dreams they can convey both approval and disapproval of actions, past, present, and future, of their descendants. In addition, dreams are held to be of both diagnostic and prognostic significance for the tribal politics and in operation of a medial system [activities that are performed jointly] — particularly where psychogenic disorders are concerned." See S.G. Lee (1958), *Social Influences*, p. 265.

psychological complexes, the bond of an arch-forefather that obligates his descendent generations, all men, to guarantee one another's offence-defense complications gained less attention. Looking at causes of empathy and antipathy among agnates, often out of the group's over-engagement with its members' intimate affairs, intense commitments to one another and their common tribal descent has drawn much less on psychological concern.

A modern philosophy of life accentuates individuality and plays down ancient perceptions that once bound us and committed us to serving our groups of descent and their cause, even if they were wrong. We are obliged to society as a whole. But why inculcate the coming generations with the belief that ego concerns are from now on the right way to go, the morally correct way?

Anthropological studies reveal a ubiquitous contrast of values accentuated in contrasting situations like: *"Il'ab la-wahdak wa tijee radhi"* (play yourself [independent of others] and come up contented), and: *"Id 'ala id – rahma"* (hand on hand [collaboration provides] mercy). These may coexist, while each expression anticipates its minute of pronouncement. Lately, Western individuality has become the street culture around rejuvenating chances of doing things one's own way.

The growing gap between the self-centered, that is, a present, "worldly" style of living and the "tribal," viz., the traditional version of running one's life, grows wider—archetypal, agnatic dreams reflect this. As though privacy is secular and tribal is a religious, adherence to the latter prevails. Once non-believers are given room for acting *inâni'* [egoist], inculcating good manners (*adab*) signifies respect for the tribe and for the tribal society at large. This was the kind of social reality in the Jawârish neighborhood at the time I worked there. Tribal ascription determined a great deal of the social leeway available to each person. As the outer social milieu opened up, the traditional one remained limiting, confining each individual to his agnatic circle. The regular flow of pedestrians and riders in the public spaces did not reveal opposition to ascription but rather surrender to ascription on occasions of feuds. Society thus prevailed. The Arabic language used at that place and that time gave much more respect to the paternal tribe than to any other social concern.

III. Psychology and Anthropology

Dreams Patterned by Cultural Issues

Psychoanalysts rightly favor evaluating their clients' problems against their immediate family and primary relations. Relatives of the first degree affect our feelings and therefore influence our behavior more than the distant ones, and the nuclear family nest is to be looked at before all distant relations. On the other hand, it is part of the social reality in the Middle East that draws attention to *'umûm* (paternal relatives) and to *ikhwâl* (maternal relatives) in different ways. The issues of tribes and of tribal ascription of clients are here of particular relevance and not only in the capacity of background detail. Knowing the potential of agnates even of a distant order to appear at once as if they were of first degree ones, when certain circumstances occur, requires caution. Susceptible to be drawn closer are chiefly *'umûm*. Rarely do *ikhwâl* come to fulfill these roles. Observing the tribe and the extended family setup alone and discovering that deep roots of paternal ascription affect the individual psyche are liable to affect one's type of dreams.

Among the Negev Bedouin dreams are rarely a matter of open discussion, a concern of men or of women in daily encounters or at social gatherings. Similar to what one can expect to find elsewhere in Israel, I have never heard dreams discussed anywhere in public events or at a *shiq*[28] assembly. Current discussions in public largely touch on matters of daily news, work conditions, markets and prices, items of community gossip and interpersonal concerns, stuff of national and international affairs and politics in general. Matters of the soul and of faith, the belief in the presence of spirits or supernatural powers, are rarely presented before a group of people. Witchcraft or sorcery are debated, but when discussed, they are often referred to as concrete analysis of world affairs, as a part of reality. Hence they are mixed in descriptions of actual occurrences, i.e., as things that had happened. Dreams or elements of things that were dreamed or the relation of dreams to reality **are** discussed, but largely as in the general society, in the form of an intimate exposure.

Help Solve Mental Problems

During my years of fieldwork among the inhabitants of the Jawârish, the Bedouin suburb of Ramle, I frequently noticed the presence of clients, mostly women, sitting waiting for a turn to meet a healer, Madame Khamisah Abu Kashef,[29] a "knowing woman," who could help them tackle feelings of depression and lasting worries, conflicts with people, especially relatives, etc. Most of these clients were women, inhabitants of other suburbs of the town. A few were her immediate neighbors, who waited at some distance, away from her door. Some of her clients sat waiting on her balcony floor.

---

[28] When the Bedouin still dwelled in nomadic tents, this was the hosting section kept for men **and guests**. Visitors arrived usually in the afternoon, would sit together on carpets spread on the floor, leaning on pillows, sip tea and coffee and talk till the early evening hours.

[29] For a mention of Khamisah Abu Kashef see Kressel, Bar Zvi & Abu Rabi'a. *The Charm of Graves* (2013), p. 174.

Khamisah, the wife of Ahmad, nicknamed "*iqtesh*,"[30] has been called "Khamisah" rather than "*mart iqtesh*." A daughter of immigrants from the Sudan, born in the Negev, she grew up in Jiser az-Zarqa,[31] and on reaching the age of 35 (an advanced age for women) was given (married off) to "the Bedouin Ahmad."

Khamisah tried at first to get a true picture of what I do or what keeps me running. Happening to see me outdoors, at first she took me for an income tax official, coming to sniff around to discover how she earns her living. Once she was accustomed to my innocuous presence, on trying to see what was on my mind she later learned from me about anthropology. That made her try to learn more about what anthropology is. Our talks became friendly. She would stop me, calling from her yard, for an exchange of information or invite me for a cup of tea.

When our talks occurred, frequently she tried testing me as one of her clients, and I was keen to respond, to talk about things of my spiritual experience and dreams and to reply to her questions, answer her inquisitive looks. Noticing my willingness to hear what she had to say about me she often tried me as a client too. Offering me her small coffee cup, for a test, she studied the coffee grounds sediment after I drank the liquid, to "read" what I feel and think as regards my world. She then guessed at the details of my immediate social surroundings, especially my family group. She did it while looking in the coffee sediment, left in my cups, based on sheer feeling. She used her intuition with me too and came close to the facts regarding my being.

At the first encounter with Khamisah, she did not request that her clients relate their trouble to her. Rather, she began the

---

[30] A nickname for a person who was born with a cleft palate.

[31] A small township by the Mediterranean shore near Haifa.

session by reading, i.e., following her intuition, what it was that had brought them to see her. Those who accepted what she had to say returned for more advice. Some let her guide them for years, accepting her suggestions for a better strategy or course of behavior. On being perplexed by personal or interpersonal problems, clients (mostly women, including Jewish ones) from the Ramle suburbs, sought her out to listen, first to diagnose what their problem was and then for her advice, what she contended to be best for them to do.

On receiving her clients, sitting with them at first, Khamisah made a practice of quietly observing their coffee cups, that is, she didn't begin with attempts at soul searching. Rather, she guessed or read what their trouble was without resorting to hypnotizing, penetrating, soul-searching looks. She softly got to the points she sensed, and slowly focused on the main ones. For touching her client's innermost problem she used intuition, then waited some time for her clients' emotions to develop. Observing her work with much interest, I felt respect for her wisdom, knowing that she was illiterate, she had barely learned to read and write, and it goes without saying that she had no psychological training and, therefore, was not authorized to function in the job she filled, a true analyst, a self-made one.

She grew to fulfill the office of an analyst by knowing how to listen and then approaching her client's problem gently. Concentrated listening and an ability to listen, read through the words she heard, she solved personal problems. On sitting in her yard waiting to see her and watching her work from the side, I noted that she never bothered to ask her clients questions such as: "What's on your mind?" Or: "What brought you over to see me?" Or: "What is your problem?" Khamisah did not interrupt her clients' talk; she did not reproach a needy person, rather let her/him realize what Allah advises them to do.

A session with Khamisah would begin when her client sat on a chair next to her and she would offer her/him a small cup (*finjân*) of bitter coffee while they exchanged niceties. On collecting the empty cup to have a look, she began to talk. Carefully reading the drying sediment of the black liquid she guessed what was on the mind of the person, the problem that brought her/him to her. Putting her clients to the test by "opening" meaning deciphered through the coffee cup (*tiftah fil finjân*), she was about to tell them as though knowing without them saying it just what their problem was.

Khamisah, the wife of "*Iqtesh*," did not have children of her own and I imagined had more time to give to her visiting clients. Indeed she was the only person around who listened to people's problems, guessing what could be on their mind although this did not include reference to clients' dreams. Khamisah typified (1968) her brand of approach by a question that was often put before her:

> "Say, what does it mean if my long deceased mother's mother all of a sudden comes talking to me and with a strict facial expression reproaches me [in a dream]?"

Being asked this question her answer would be:

> "It can be the result of disobeying this grandmother's tradition. Isn't it? Question is what did the old lady mean for the teller, of course." And she had more to say:

Dreams rarely tell things in a straightforward manner and people rarely talk of what they saw while asleep in a straightforward manner. More often while amassing memories that come in a roundabout manner the result is nonsense. Noting that she did not inquire about clients' dreams, all the more so in consideration of their use of time, made me respect her sincerity. Khamisah reminded me of a known analyst with whom I was familiar, who had learned something about dreams and therefore, or nonetheless, belittled the practice of making them the subject matter in the therapeutic process.

How to Treat the Mentally Troubled?

There were few people with professional expertise available for the psychological treatment of patients in both fields of my studies, in the Jawârish neighborhood of Ramle and in the Negev Highlands. For *ad hoc* help, the needy were directed to clinics in town. From the knowledge I obtained of anecdotes related to traditional healers they did not dwell on analysis of dreams. The healing process dwells on the rapport the patients have with their fate and Allah and with their relatives, thus talking of normative propriety and of deviation (not indeed sins) provide the main line of the talks. Shaking the victim out of a demon's clutches implied a harsh physical treatment accompanied with frightening hollering to scare it out.

Traditional healers were not dream decipherers or soul-searching specialists. As experts they did not pay attention to the sphere that modern psychology would call the "unconscious" to be revealed by means of their patients' dream material. Rather their performance seemed similar to those of medicine men who also employ non-verbal devices to heal the needy, i.e., those who have largely been harmed by an "evil eye."[32]

---

[32] An "evil eye" has several definitions following different practices observed by ethnographers. Malevolent activities that intend to harm others by means of demons are defined as sorcery. Mishaps can occur, as believed, also due to jealousy that does not reach the awareness of those who activate it. In this case the individuals who are taken to be the cause of bad luck remain unaware of their "guilt." It is the harmed party who brings it to their awareness, often even paying them homage to pacify evil.

Perceptions of an evil eye I use here is the consequence of jealousy, no more than the wishful feeling to have the success, the position or the possessions of someone else, which can cause that person damage. The sudden damage that occurred to A brought about a search for a culprit who, due to her or his objective poverty, might have caused it, even if unintentionally, so that the damage occurred.

Unlike sorcery that indicates the manipulation of objects and/or whispers, i.e., prayers meant to harm the fate of others, helped by supernatural powers, witchcraft (after Evans-Pritchard, 1937)[33] explains misfortune that can occur out of jealousy alone. In accordance with Evans-Pritchard, the mind of A sees him or herself placed in an inferior position relative to B. B may be wholly unaware of A and, nevertheless, B's physical traits, personal background or successful deeds cause A to be angry, the source of which she or he is unaware of, that hurt his or her self image. Then B may become for A the object of jealousy and a target of "retribution" for "crimes" he did not commit.

For the people among whom I spent long periods of fieldwork the meanings of the evil eye were obvious and a common explanation for misfortune. An expression often heard was: — "*Eyn al xasûd lâ bitsûd,*" which means, "the jealous eye won't rule." On the whole, the charge of B for causing an evil eye act was related to a third person, C. This category, it occurred to me, included myself too. An approach to the one suspected of witchcraft can lead to a denial and more, to a crisis. Rather, it was related to C along with a request to act as go-between.

As I heard from my acquaintances, traditional healers were to be found beyond immediate reach. A few were to be found in distant locations, either because of the belief in expertise nourished in

---

[33] See as well *Notes and Queries on Anthropology* (1960), pp. 188-189.

its natural "flower bed" (i.e., not near the sophisticated medical institutions of Israel), or distrust toward those who live nearby, due to them being partial or biased. During the 1960s and 1970s both in the Jawârish neighborhoods and among the Negev Bedouin in my acquaintance the needy turned to healers in the Gaza Strip. Most of these healers did not depend on a clientele from next door. In addition, from the summer of 1967, few of the knowledgeable healers from Gaza had arrived to treat the Negev needy. In Gaza and its environs those extracting demons out of the "disturbed" were mostly elders, men and a few women.

Upon facing serious psychological problems, inhabitants of the Jawârish neighborhoods, most of them insured properly, turned to the nearby hospitals.[34] The Negev Bedouin resorted to the Beersheva Mental Health Center or to the Soroka Hospital Psychiatric Department, which is largely their first choice. The general hospital accepts the needy even prior to settling bureaucratic concerns. Both these hospitals employ a considerable number of Arab staff, which is helpful when dealing with the Bedouin clientele. In cases of acute disturbance the Negev Bedouin approach clinics run by West Bank monasteries and the Bethlehem Psychiatric Asylum, too, where both European and local (Arab) personnel work. Often the doctors of both groups are not acquainted with the Bedouin code of behavior, customs and manners. However, acquaintance with the normative for the broad Arab society is taken into consideration in choosing "total institutions,"[35] once families are in need of hospitalization for a mentally ill family member.

Neither the Israeli nor the Palestinian medical institutions allow traditional healers or healers employing methods of the distant past in their premises. It occasionally occurs that clergymen

---

[34] The regional hospitals are Assaf Ha-Rofe and Shmuel Ha-Rofe.
[35] After Erving Goffman's concept of - "Total Institutions" (1957).

come to comfort hospitalized individuals and pray for people's sanity, as well as some intervention by alternative medical methods. Men in the position of *imâm*[36] or *ma'dhûn*[37] are seen at hospitals, largely alongside the visiting family members. Being familiar with holy texts they are requested to pacify the mentally disturbed, praying to Allah — and nothing more.

For moderate or less extreme mental concerns, prior to hospitalization, healers employing traditional methods are beseeched. I had the opportunity to observe some healers at work while they treated patients. I was allowed to sit silently in the background of the tent's *shiq* and observe. A healer in Rahat[38] has the reputation of having a diagnostic ability, to see through and tell the causes of "light mental disorders," like anorexia nervosa,[39] that in accordance with his clients can be cured without the use of drastic medical devices (so he says).

This taught me how to treat the source of trouble thus neutralizing disturbing factors by moderate means, avoiding external, intrusive methods. Each client was met at first by a diagnostic test that is "opening by means of coffee cups" (*el-fatx bel-finjân*). Based on the findings the healer moved on, acting to distance the demons causing the trouble, to hold off the victim's soul. In accordance with a widespread belief, *Jinni* (sig. *jinn*), meaning demons that are perceived as the source of mental disturbance, are clever enough to enjoy every minute

---

[36] One who leads the caravan and hence figuratively is a moral guide, or the leader of the congregation in prayer.

[37] A clergy who is authorized to register marrying and divorcing couples.

[38] He requested to remain anonymous. Rahat is the largest (40,000 inhabitants) Bedouin town in the Negev, situated some 12 miles north of Be'er Sheva.

[39] An eating disorder characterized by immoderate food restriction and irrational fear of gaining weight.

in their victim's mind. Methods are needed to lure them out. The inventory of temptations meant for *jinn* included tasty drinks, inhaling of sweet smelling smoke, light massage that tickles them, thus easing their hold, or stepping barefoot on the client's back that surprises them. All means in the healer's toolkit are meant to frighten and astound these cunning, evil human souls, who live off of other people's possessions. The healing process includes using all possible means pulling, luring or scaring the demons away.[40]

In a Bedouin Quarter in Town

In the spring of 1966 I began to study the new neighborhoods of the town of Ramle, in the center of Israel, which at that time was home to some 35,000 residents. My interest brought me mainly to the Bedouin quarter of the town where former herders were becoming acquainted with an urban way of life. All local labor markets required retraining and readjustment to different kinds of jobs. Modern concrete homes came to replace former accommodations. New patterns of social organization forced coexistence with other groups of inhabitants and with the municipal service departments. Authorities were elected rather than traditional councils of elders. The surrounding social life thus called for reorganization. Obligatory schooling for both boys and girls limited the employment of under-aged youngsters in family work. With that, patterns of consumption took on the town's ways, first for men then also for women. First, the growing demand for know-how and for authorized diplomas now preconditioned promotion at work and increased investment in schooling, mainly for boys but

---

[40] Devices such as pieces of aluminum sulfate (shaving stone) are used, that when put in a fire metamorphose, giving the impression of disappearing, "evaporates the evil = the wrong." See Kressel, Bar Zvi & Abu Rabi'a (2013), *The Charm of Graves,* Chapter 4.

then also for girls. Customary cultural styles were modified following development and environmental change.

However, a few patterns of thinking survived and have had an effect on the present social system. The main one is the lasting adherence to tribal frameworks. One's core agnation still preserves an infrastructure of extended families and of tribes that to an outside observer becomes apparent with intra-tribal conflicts.[41] Social change does not occur suddenly. Keen observation of urbanization throughout the Middle East and in comparison to these processes elsewhere indicates the lasting hold of pre-urban patterns of association. The relative importance of tribal ascription may diminish to an extent but nevertheless survives the transition. Growing into urban life necessitates associating with alternative, voluntary groups of different kinds, along with or instead of one's group of agnates. Despite the syllogism based on experience gathered from similar world processes, an on-going replacement of pre-urban grouping by new ones occurs in a slow and hesitant transition. Dictates of paternal ascription predominate the infrastructure of the Middle Eastern cultural arena.

A Word on Method

Attention to the telling of dreams has not been part of my academic agenda,[42] but rather an interest. Hearing

---

[41] See Kressel (1996). *Ascendancy Through Aggression.*

[42] My training included Middle Eastern studies and sociology for my first degrees, then cultural and social anthropology for my graduate degrees. Together with these I was interested in micro-economy, work conditions and earning a living, on the one hand, and uses of money, i.e., patterns of consumption, on the other hand. Marketing patterns and open market days engaged me for years, following the methods of bargaining in the Bedouin market in Be'er Sheva.

acquaintances or friends wishing to relate to me the details of a dream they had finds me ready to sit down and listen. I began reading psychology prior to my university training, though as a student I was interested in social psychology more than in psychology proper. Years later I learned about the view of dreams as a message coming from the unconscious. Some may be born with a better sensitivity needed to read through their own unconscious revelations, but not so are most of us, whose familiarity with the psychic codes and the way to decipher them are aided by psychoanalysts.

I learned about the role of psychoanalysis in bringing the deciphered essence of patients' dreams to their awareness discussing my own dream material with Dr. R. Schärf-Kluger and Dr. Y. H. Kluger, my mother's sister and her husband, who studied under Professor C.G. Jung in Zurich. Both were practicing analysts in Los Angeles during the years 1962-1965 when I attended UCLA[43] studying cultural anthropology. I did not follow their path to become an analyst, although I was enriched, thanks to them, with means I had not thought about before, in the search for what is actually presented to us in our dream material. Learning the psyche mode of expressing innermost feelings, when in conflict with our overt, conscious position, sharpened my thinking about that which relates the dreams people face to their actual problems.

A basic and constant feature of Middle Eastern culture, giving the impression of a meme,[44] is not a simple pattern of adaptation to environmental conditions always on the verge of re-adaptation, facing change of a physical setting. To explain the "tribal complex" special tools are needed in addition to

---

[43] The University of California Los Angeles.

[44] A meme is an idea that is passed on from one human generation to another. It is the cultural equivalent of a gene, the basic element of biological inheritance.

societal ones. On undertaking a study of traits that mark the region's infrastructure, regardless of the environment, be it in the town or in the desert, and in people's dreams, the use of some psychology is necessary.

On noting patterns of paternal Sheikhs appearing in dreams, I reread the works of Freud (1953) and Jung (1963), with their two different sorts of dream analysis. Both attempted to make their clients aware of or closely relate to their psyche about what their dreams revealed. Deciphering dreams was for each of them slightly different, e.g., "subconscious" for Freud was "unconscious" for Jung, and various reasons were provided to explain it, while they were both attentive to the revelation of what was hidden though essential in dreams for their patients, a precondition to recovery.

Social and Psychological

In order to tackle the dream material selected from my notebooks, I put to work both social and psychological analytical measures, a merger of tools suited to treat the two dimensions appropriate to this case study. The "tribal meme," once the sole business of social studies, relates to the automatic logic of a physical adaptation, which disregards its tenacity through time and space. Explaining a pattern of behavior by social adaptation assumes its transmission from one generation to another thanks to its ecological merits, in spite of changing environmental conditions. The tribe may be the proper organizational device for living in deserts and living in towns, a lasting feature of the social structure through the last millennia, and its very presence evinces value. Subscribing to such an attitude hinders the attempt to evaluate what keeps this "practice" alive.

The prevalence of old agnates in the telling of dreams aroused my interest to focus on persons to whom these stories were addressed. There were those who thanked the dreamer for telling about the dream, and listened to their non-social affairs, those who ask me to please note their dream, provided that it was prophetic or crucial to the future. For others it was important to hear what I had to say, broadly speaking, and also, often, in reference to details: "What can you see is the contribution of these details to revelation as a whole?"

On being asked for my opinion about a dream or relevance of its details, I tried to explain what I knew about the language of dreams, in general, and to add my thoughts as regards the particular dream I had just heard about. It occurred once in a while that a question was addressed to me: "Why is the significant message of dreams hidden, or, how can I distinguish the main bit from the other features which are secondary in importance?" To answer a question about the hidden "play" or the disguised bit of a dream, or why it doesn't speak in a straightforward manner, my explanation was that the reason is unknown to me, and I added that this is the nature of things. To accord a dream a divine purpose would suggest that thus Allah tests us, granting the Divine a pedagogical plan, for which we lack proof. However, the more we learn to follow the course of dreams and read what they are saying the more we can rightly marvel on nature's creation that resembles finding a medicine to cure an illness.

Most conversations concerning the nature of dreams were raised by men, though women told me of dreams they had too. Mention of tribal elders appearing in dreams was common, often followed by the question of why they keep on visiting their descendants in dreams. Frequent also and familiar in dreams was the encounter with an angry elder, his look stern as though he had come to reproach the dreamer who confronts him. On the whole, the impression was that those long deceased elders, speaking or silent in their descendants' dreams, appeared to reproach or to transfer a feeling of guilt.

Noting all that they put before me, including dreams, brought people to check my ability to resolve their concerns about disturbing, partly spiritual, themes of dreams. A case in point that made the dreamers wish to share an experience with someone who could say something knowledgeable was in regards to the visits of Sheikhs in dreams.

I was attentive to applicants in a face-to-face manner, largely standing outdoors. People stopped me, starting with a prolonged exchange of greetings. Talks that led to a thick (rich) description caused us to kneel (*'a* [*'ala*]-*qimbez*), and for me to take note of things I heard, leading to sitting on the ground alongside one another. Rather than sitting comfortably on chairs, in a room, sitting sideways made it informal, unofficial. Meeting in the open, I learned, could attract other listeners, mostly children, but less so when it occurred *'a* [*'ala*]-*qimbez*. Unlike with actual analysts, including Khamisah, in their work sessions, to support my words explaining the nature of dreaming I gave my narrator examples from my own dream experience. Feeling free I entrusted material from my own intimate world routinely to manifest mutuality.

The path of a social scientist and an occasional advisor as regards dreams seemed to better fit my approach. It felt correct in terms of my position and expressed a kind of good will to listen to social concerns the people have and often to their dreams as well. Being acknowledged as a university person conferred respect as a knowledgeable person, also as regards psychology. Answering dream questions outdoors did not reduce my standing but rather placed me, so I felt, on an amateur or semi-professional ground.

Attempting to show the connection between what actually happens to us during the day and the dream was often accomplished through use of my personal experience, which, I believed, limited similarity between my answers and the enigmatic ones of any imagined physician. A tolerant listener, I availed myself of stories, and was thus approached by acquaintances repeatedly as they returned to me, requesting to hear what I had to say about the last dream they had, time and again.

Choosing instances out of my learning kit and my dream material obliged me to pay further attention to match my words to each person. Using my own material for an answer added the risk of reducing the effect of what I said. I had to frame my words so as to help, not hurt the feelings of the supplicants asking for advice. In addition, on indicating a vector leading from our daily experiences to our psyche, reflected in dreams, implied trivializing the role played by Allah. A careful choice of words then became important to demonstrate how current affairs may have an impact on both the conscious and the subconscious in different ways at the same time. Questions such as how to demonstrate the relatedness of mind and matter and be convincing occupied my thoughts in preparing for another day of fieldwork.

Along with dream descriptions, I heard about conceptions people had as to how dreams occur in our minds. A frequent belief was to see the dream as a supernatural act. Conceivably Allah provokes in us these reminders for a second thought, to reconsider dubious things we do, or wrongly perform, thus we are corrected, perhaps encouraged to take a better course. Or, we become aware of things we would rather do, instead of doing nothing, i.e., that we avoid doing, being too obedient or overly shy, with no justification.

If so, then why must the assessment of things we do, right or wrong, be conveyed to us particularly while we are asleep? Thinking it is a product of the psyche rather than of some external intervention indicates exposure to an inner resistance that goes on in us, based on feelings aroused in us despite an overt conviction. Something in us expresses doubt about overt attitudes we have, contrary to the obvious, an inner reservation that could be convincing on a daily basis, or encouraging us when we avoid doing things while overwhelmed with fear. Inner disagreement with overt agreement may come as an alarm or a challenge urging us to reconsider whatever we do or the way we behave.

Habitual listening to people's dreams revealed similarities despite their extensive range of educational and intellectual horizons. Differences in intellect were apparent although not in flavor or color or pitch. Also, I became aware of systemic differences, the function of attention to and consideration of their speech. Various people had varying experiences but, nevertheless, the dream features were similar and pointed to a quality that required an answer to a particular need.

To the best of my memory my dreams were not visited by images of instructive forefathers. Rarely had I heard about a scolding or warning grandpa, either maternal or paternal, who came to me in my dreams. A search for a message, providing a way out of predicaments I faced, came from other directions, pointing at alternative sources of wisdom. However, relying on my own dream material enabled me to discuss the encoded language of other people's dreams and refer to them as messages of their unconscious. I often could suggest ideas of relief from fears, a reason to alleviate worries or hardship, solve predicaments — providing optimism as a promising key to the future.

On returning to these cases, rereading my notebooks again, now, forty years after I wrote them, I could put aside a great deal of the context as well as the references to talks of dreams and ideas as to the nature of dreaming. Isolating the pronouncements of Sheikhs in dreams by anecdotes distinguished the generation and age of the persons receiving them or whether the recipients were women or men. I preferred presenting those dreams that indicated a social or tribal contextual meaning, putting aside individual concerns or implications of purely personal affairs. Though interesting, some of the personal references were of a kind that identifies the individual. Often, also, the personal dimension indicated issues of important [group, i.e., tribal concerns] meanings.

IV. Archetypal Dreams of an Agnatic Order

Forefathers in Dreams

The concept of a great Father, related to an imagined masculine God, is shared by the monotheist creeds and, to an extent, by the other world religions.[45] Matching figures of deities as imagined by different people belong to the field of comparative religions. Somewhere in a place beyond the heavens there is a room for a prototype or primordial image of the Father that is pre-existent and supra ordinate to all phenomena in which the "paternal" in the broadest sense of the term is manifest.

Included here are descriptions of dreams told in my presence or to me personally that portray the appearance of a paternal figure, usually a forefather, an old Sheikh, commonly viewed is a man known to the dreamer who lived generations ago and who is considered to be the founding father of the tribe. The image of his stature thus relates his descendents to one another by virtue of "having one blood" running in their veins. Founding forefathers' names are given to their descendants and identify them jointly. Naming the entire lineage after their primordial father happens in the capacity of him as the tribe's creator primogenitor and the reason for their relatedness to one another. I choose to place the following talk of dreams

---

[45] See e.g., *The Teaching of Buddha* (1960). Tokyo: Kōaido Printing. *Srimad Bhagavadgita* (1999). Gorakhpur: Gita Press.

in chronological order, as they occurred and as I wrote them down in my notebooks.

Dreams Where a Paternal Sheikh Emerges: Tell and Foretell

Dream Teller 1: Dreams are not in Vain

1. a. Aminah 'A.

Aminah 'A. (31), a housewife and a mother of six, quotes for me the saying of her mother (58), who explained to her the nature of dreams and the sense in their appearing to us.

> "Dreams are not in vain; they appear as though like a haze, for no apparent reason, but they do have a purpose.[46] Mind what you've seen when asleep and give it your attention. The question for us is what to do about calling a dream back once we are awake. The dream of last night isn't always clear in the morning. Recalling it before it fades away takes another minute of concentration after sleep. Do it when your eyes are still closed."

> "Though dreams can be elusive, my mother contends that they are worth our attention, meaning for us to give them thought, think about what they show. Do you [Gideon] mind your dreams as to memorize them?"

---

[46] For an inconsistent reference to dreams, once seen as a vanity and respected as messages from the Divine in the Bible, see the wording of Zechariah 10; 2: —"For the idols have spoken vanity and the diviners have seen a lie, and have told false dreams; they comfort in vain…"

— When I get up in haste it happens that I don't. But when I have the time, that's it, on getting up with peace of mind like on a quiet Saturday morning, then I do and largely take notes about the dream I had.

"My mother has an idea as regards the elements shown in her dreams. She knows how to decipher their meaning, be it as comments that regard her present day or as regards the days to come. For instance, once in her sleep she was shown a ripe fig, an open plum, a strawberry, watermelon and so on, also a simple soft boiled egg, she was saying, 'I should better be ready for the appearance of wickedness; a harsh, annoying day is before me. I shall better be ready because it will surely come. Things will occur to agitate me but knowing it in advance can keep me calm.'"

"Another sign of alarm she takes into consideration for example is when her eyelashes start trembling. For her it indicates a time to immediately relax. It foretells that she should sit down and take a deep breath before she rises up. Once she is ready for a day of annoyance she doesn't get too excited; she is patient with whatever comes with the slightest sign of unrest. One of the measures she takes is the placing of a piece of straw on her eyebrow to serve her as a reminder. It serves as a nerve watch. Did you [Gideon] hear something about these measures, when they appear in our dreams?"[47]

— I cannot add much as regards the fruit images you have just mentioned. I don't know what they might signify when they appear, either one after the other or together. In fact I don't

---

[47] See Goldberg & Admon (2003). *The Giant Dictionary for Dreams' Interpretation*.

recall having dreamed about them. It didn't occur to me. Can you ask to hear more from your mother about it? A general idea of these fruits and what they might stand for once come into a night dream is hard to tell. They can mean different things on different occasions, even for a single person. I can refer the question to experts [I thought of Drs. R. S. Kluger and Y. H. Kluger].

> "By the side of Nabi Sâleh [a grave of a *wali*, contemporary of the Prophet Muhammad in the town of Ramle], some days during the year, persons knowing how to read dreams arrive. The graves of *Shuyukh* [plural of *Sheikh*] are suitable for their work. By *awliyâ* [sing. a *wali*] graves to be found are those who can tell the hidden in dreams. They consult the [deceased] *wali* who tells them what the dreamer needs to know."

Belief that the meaning of dreams can be explained by *awliyâ*, who receive it by consulting Allah, mean dreams are an act of the Divine. On the other hand, dreaming of fruit indicates a secular code of interpretation. Following a second thought I added:

— Traits common to all the items your mother mentioned, once appearing in dreams, is their watery, somewhat crimson or yellow look. Ripe fruit and soft vegetables have those qualities, don't they? They are largely juicy.

> Aminah 'A: "Indeed, my mother says that in case nuts appear in a dream [not watery, not soft] they are a healthier sign. Once nuts are seen, the dream can indicate the arrival of a positive outcome."

— Does your mother have a particular person, someone with whom she prefers to discuss her thoughts once interesting dreams occur to her?

"She has her friends and acquaintances and, also, *awliyâ,* who keep on coming while she is asleep, are exponents (*wustâa*) who help her to interpret dreams."

— Is your mother particular about the dream interpreters she consults in accordance with the kind of dream she had? Is her experience with the acquaintances coming to consult her? Try to ask for her interpretation about their dreams? Does a *wali* appear along with a night dream, or maybe the *awliyâ* come into view only afterward, once we ponder the meaning of a passing dream, to explain to us what it has to tell us?

"Once a *wali* [always an elderly, bearded man] appears in her dream she takes it as a sign that her dream has a particular importance. Don't you also see your grandfathers in the dreams you have?"

— I find it difficult to recall a time they appeared in my dreams. To answer this question frankly, it seems I did dream about them and forgot about it. My mother's father died before I was born. My father's father died when I was twelve years old. I loved this grandpa dearly. He would tell me stories. For years after his death I still missed talking to him and in a sense feel longing for him until now. He was not a binding authority for me. I grew up in a kibbutz where our teachers were the meaningful instructors more than our parents. I saw my parents only for a few afternoon hours and our grandparents we saw even less. Besides, my father's father who was very close to me didn't have particular features such as a long beard and his voice was soft. He rarely raised his voice.

My words were heard with care and let the discussion flow. Aminah thought about my mother's father who died months before my birth. She noted that much was different between her customs and mine regarding the two sets of grandfathers we had. Aminah had been brought up to respect her paternal grandparents and less so her maternal ones.[48]

1. b. A Supplement to Last Week's Talk

Cultural rather than psychological differences and personal experience seemed to be the difference between the two of us on seeing either a paternal or a maternal grandparent in a dream. This was vitally indicative of two traditions, the one Aminah's and the other mine, that provided material for thought. In addition to personal differences of preference stood the inculcated distinction of consanguine relatives, that so interested me. Weighing it on an anthropological level revealed a further case of differing elements in dreaming. Then an occasion for talk with Aminah occurred, as follows.

A week after our first talk, Aminah turned to me to add things and emphasize others, pointing at aspects she wanted me to re-write, particularly as regards her mother's understanding of dreams:

> "My mother contends that on seeing one's elder [deceased father or father's father] in a dream this is to oblige you to go and visit him [his grave]. A man may feel obliged to sacrifice on his elder's grave in an additional act to the usual sacrifice once a year, on the *khamis al mawât* [the Thursday of the Dead at the end of the Ramadan month]."

— Would seeing your father's mother [who died in 1957, some ten years earlier] in a dream oblige you to pay her a visit, go to her grave too?

---

[48] On the difference between the maternal and paternal kin in Middle Eastern society see W. Robertson Smith (1903).

"I think [i.e., logically] yes, but I am not sure about it. I must talk to my mother about it. People are devoted alike to the memory of both their late parents but as regards their grandparents, I think, our commitment to the maternal ones is not as necessary. It's less obliging."

One is more committed to devotion to *'umûm,* i.e., relatives through the father's side, than to *ikhwâl,* who are the relatives through the mother. Though both are consanguine relatives, even if of a first degree, individuals are brought up to feel less commitment and cherished love for *ikhwâl,* including their mother's parents as compared to their *'umûm* for whom respect is obligatory.

Teller 2. 'A. Al-Salâm; Dreams Facilitate Admission and Repentance: Learning the Hard Way

Following are the dreams of 'Abd Al-Salâm (29), a construction contractor, married and a father of three, a man who hadn't given much value to talk about dreams and not paid attention to his own until he happened to change his mind as regards the potential of dreams, once in jail for a fortnight, where by chance he met a dream diviner.

A Few Words on the Meaning of Dreams

'Abd Al-Salâm[49] speaks about the knowledge he gained about the meaning of dreams. He then brought before me, for my attention, a few dreams he had had several months earlier and the other night, asking me to reflect on them as observed

---

[49] Fieldnotes 1968 (pp. 191-192).

from the peculiar kind of outlook I had. 'Abd Al-Salâm asks for my opinion:

> "What should a dream mean to you? Does it come to tell you something new or something of importance you didn't know? If some dreams are yes and some are not telling, then how would you know? Once they are no more than a trifle or planted in our heads to indicate a mental disturbance (*'iz'âdj*), no more, there is no sign for it. Some other dreams call for more attention. They can be a warning or a sign of something of importance that you are about to go through. But how would you tell the **sort** of the dream you have had? What counts as important enough to call our attention [or forget about it]? The second kind carries a warning or calling for your attention. It comes to prepare you for fulfillment (*'ixaâ*). It comes to the dreamer as prophetic (*tanabb'u*). It comes to awaken us hence to let us have time to get ready before the trouble occurs. As if the Angel Jibreel [Gabriel] comes to wake you on time."

2. a. Once in jail

> "When in jail[50] I saw in a dream myself on a boat, sailing deep into the sea. In the morning I told of this ship to Sheikh 'Adel [dream interpreter who happened to be in jail together with him] who said that being on a ship stands for being in jail. You can't just leave it and go. The sea around stands for the country's law or the government [that removes us from home], taking our freedom away. But the sail implies as well that it will soon come to a shore."

---

[50] A-S spent two weeks in jail following an attempt to cross the international border after the Six Day War.

2. b. My father talks

"In my second dream I saw my father [who died a few years earlier] watching me digging, the minute I reached and hit a water pipe that was covered there. A wild stream came out of it and drenched me all over. I then dug around to fix the damage. My dad watched me with a content expression. Agreeing with me. I told about it [the dream] to the Sheikh 'Adel who interpreted the dream saying: — 'You know your father didn't agree with you, jeopardizing your freedom and in fact, risking your life [by crossing the border], while it was your responsibility to work, because you must provide food for your children."

The first dream relates 'Abd Al-Salâm's state of mind from a sphere [open sea] he had never experienced before. His impression of sailing he got from some movies he saw. However, the second dream relates 'Abd Al-Salâm to his routine work and to a situation in which he repairs a fault he created while in a construction job, which he later repaired. He is shown able to surmount the trouble and undo the damage caused by him earlier.

2. c. My Father's Father talks

"I had a third dream, in fact a short one when in jail.[51] My father's father [pensive], or was it another elder of

---

[51] He tried to sneak across the Jordan River to 'Amman. From the Hashemite Kingdom of Jordan he planned on reaching Wurfallah [a town, the capital of a district in Libya], the land of his Bedouin forefathers. He was caught by the Israeli border police and imprisoned.

our family, appeared to me in tears and crying he told me: 'It is time for you to get married.'"

Sheikh 'Adel: "Your grandfather was crying while facing you because you put your life in jeopardy, lest he will see you die before your time, for a childish, unjustifiable cause."

The man, 'Abd Al-Salâm, who was by then married and a father of three, had been asked in this dream to get married again, perhaps meaning to beget more children, which in accordance with Islam is permitted. He asked for my opinion of the interpretation he received for this dream in jail.

— I suggested that his grandfather's words are not necessarily a request that he remarry but rather mature in the sense of to **fulfill** his marriage and obligations of fatherhood, *viz.*, stay with his loved ones, responsible enough, i.e., not venture, wasting money and efforts, and all the more, not put his life in danger.

'Abd Al-Salâm, altering my words as regards his original version: "Perhaps my father [who died a few years earlier, buried in Ramle and his grave had rarely been visited since] calls me to pay a visit and sacrifice a sheep at his grave's foot [for his spirit, i.e., the dead man acts not out of concern for the living but out of a selfish concern for the respect he receives from his offspring]. He calls on them to cherish his memory, rather than follow their worldly concerns, minding their business alone."

— On seeing your father's father's image in a dream and hearing him talk, it may be that your *nafs* [soul, psyche], perhaps, projects thus intentions to your [deceased] grandfather. It is your view of your deceased grandfather, the way he is in **your** mind, not vice versa [you on his mind]. He is between you and you. What he tells you is in fact what you had of his admonishing words when he was still alive, things he said were part of your recollection, that come to change the things you do wrong now, in light of his words.

Curious to test the validity of my approach 'Abd Al-Salâm mentioned another dream he had a few months earlier, before the weeks he spent in jail: —

2. d. Into the depths of the open sea

"I saw I was sailing on a vessel that was heading far into the depths of the open sea, further and further away. That was all. No indication afterwards what had happened to me. When in jail I related this previous dream to Sheikh 'Adel, that roommate I told you about, a man of about 50 years old, to whom also the other men approached on having disturbing dreams. He listened to me and said: 'That ship in this context is this jail, i.e., the government is the sea around us that is confining us here; it doesn't let us go freely to wherever we please.' Can you [G] confirm this interpretation?"

Asking for my opinion, if I could add to the words of Sheikh 'Adel, the dream diviner in jail, I suggested the following:

— Being placed as a sailor, far away from home, this dream expresses dissatisfaction with the daily or a wish to extract yourself from the regular set up [family life included]; perhaps it reflects a preference to get free from the "golden chains," or maybe the yoke in your feeling is the burden of your family of origin that bothers you. Isn't it sometimes a burden? But by joining your loyalties to the group of your wandering tribesmen and the liberated elders of the tribal past you forsake your wife and the little children, shake free of responsibility.

My suggestion was accepted in silence. Not commenting on my suggestion, 'Abd Al-Salâm thought of the dream he had in reference to his attitude or the correction of attitude, shaking free of commitment to his wife and children, and tried to test my interpretation compared to another dream he had of his grandfather, that Sheikh 'Adel resolved for him during those weeks in jail.

When I stopped, again, 'Abd Al-Salâm asked a question: "So what can you [Gideon] add about my dream and its interpretation by Sheikh 'Adel the dream diviner?"

Following my words, summing up my thoughts as regards the last dream, 'Abd Al-Salâm addressed me with another dream story that was ready for the telling, as though he had prepared it ahead of time:

2. e. I saw my late Grandfather

"I saw my grandfather or was it my own father, another time in my sleep, an event about which I told the dream diviner, in the presence of our five cellmates in jail, asking for his solution to what I'd seen: —

A water pipe broke beneath the surface of the ground and a stain of wet spread, reaching our [family] eyes. It aroused everybody's concern. I took up a pick and a hoe and dug for the pipe and uncovered the crack. I worked hard, removed the earth, till a splash of water spurted out. I fixed the pipe, sealed the hole in it, as my father watched me work, wordless. Lifting my head I then realized that the entire community was watching.

The interpreter [Sheikh 'Adel] listened to me and said: 'Another day or two and they [the jail guard] will release you and let you go home.' So it was. He knew what was about to come based on my words [dream context]. By my dream he could read what would happen."

— After all you committed no crime. It seems your elders [deceased grandfather and father alike] saw you and heard you well to understand that your repentance is an innermost act. No need to torture yourself more for the mistake you made, which is enough. You were only about to do and thus made him guess they [the police] had no reason to feed you any longer on the account of the taxpayers [keep you in jail], knowing you can earn your bread, meaning to allow you to return home soon.

Dream Teller 3. Salmân Hazâz Disturbed by Encompassing Middle Eastern Scenes That Create Personal Agitation

Salmân Hazâz (36), an agricultural worker, lived with his family in two caravans near the side road connecting Ramle and Rehovot, by the Jawârish neighborhood. Salmân was the husband of two wives, each one having her own caravan.[52] The following dreams were related to me in two phases that evolved in the following manner:

Salmân saw me walking and greeting me loudly, summoning me to join him for a cup of tea in his home's yard. While sitting together he asked for my consideration to help him make sense out of an unsettling riddle he faced from a dream he had. "Please come and hear me and tell me what it means, can you, for ten minutes not more?"

---

[52] December 1967, following the Six Day War of the summer of that year (notes 328-334).

— "Of course," I said. I accepted his invitation to listen, but a problem arose at home and he was called by one of his wives for help, and the duty made him excuse himself and he left.

We met again two days later, happening to be walking the side road of this neighborhood, alongside one another. Salmân said: "*sudfa wa la mi'et mi'âd*! [encounter by mere chance is better than one hundred appointments]. We began talking while sitting *'a gimbez* [kneeling] to let him relate to me "a very personal matter." Later we set on the ground for a long hour.

These dreams engaged Mr. Hazâz both regarding a personal problem and regarding a bewildering national one, meaning the future relationships of Arab-Muslims and Jews in the country [Israel] and the Middle East in general. These two issues occupied his thoughts and his dreams intermingled, on several levels as follows:

3. a. Time before the War of June 1967

"A year ago [seven months before the war of June 1967 i.e., the Six Day War] I went to sleep angry. I am constantly in anger because we have no luck because time goes by and we beget no children. I saw the stars and the moon in the dark skies. Some stars then began to fall. A few surprisingly ricochetted back from earth to the skies again. Others were bouncing up and down, then arranged in two long lines. I ran away like everybody around me, until we reached a group of bearded men sitting in tents. They were wearing goatskins, roasting goats' meat. They were in a laughing mood. Young, half naked women moved among them. We listened to them self-assured, talking politics. I warned them saying: 'behave yourselves, next year a war is about to start and we [Arabs] are about to lose it. Most of them, more than half of them, firmly objected to letting me talk and the other few said quietly that they didn't believe me, but didn't stop me talking. Only the hosting Sheikh repeated what he heard me say, using my words: 'Maybe yes this war is worthless, and maybe not.' And taking my words he left me silently, just leaving the doubts I had unresolved."[53]

This dream story had placed the teller and his people in a primordial setting among stone-age people but they were a clever folk, amid a "star war" setting. As it was told the chances of following what happened were limited. In the same breath came the second dream story, as it related to the first one and to me:

3. b. A month before the war

"A month before the war [viz. early May 1967] I dreamed I was asleep in this barrack of mine. Midnight arrived and suddenly I heard a knock on my door. I opened my eyes and saw two giants, maybe of three meters high each, who said to me: 'Get dressed and come out with us.' So I did and the outside of my barrack seemed different, altogether different than the way our place here looks. We entered into a big mountain and the door closed behind us, leaving us in darkness."

— Had it been a cave like, e.g., the one of 'Ali Baba and his forty thieves'? Did the cave in the mountain seemed like it swallowed them or a closed-in shelter [archetypal womb[54]], to

---

[53] December 1966.

[54] The cave is the place of rebirth, that secret cavity in which one is shut up in order to be incubated and renewed. The Koran says of it: "You might have seen the rising sun decline to the right of their cavern, and as it set, go past them on the left, while they [the Seven Sleepers] stayed in the middle." See Jung (1972): Ch. 3, pp. 69-81.

be used as a hiding place, or for training, forging a military force? Could it suggest a hiding place for a clandestine army, getting ready to reappear and strike by surprise?

"No, there inside, at once it was all quiet. There was no sign of war or of a training army excitement. A big Sheikh King [*Malik*][55] and two big guards sat there next to one another. The King got up to receive me as a guest of honor, made me sit next to him. Then many men came in, intending to show themselves as though they were injured coming to a hospital. They entered niches made out of straw and lay down on straw beds, in the cave.

The treatment for the first who contracted cancer includes a cut in the neck out of which the bad blood was extracted and a new kind of good blood was infused, together with garlic juice for disinfection [resembling antibiotics]. The second man had diabetes. His blood was removed and instead he was given turtle's blood that is a promise of many years of life. The third man in the row slept. He seemed Jewish. I asked about him but the Doctor said that it is forbidden to identify the patients' ascription.

We entered another room where at the center was a big pile of straw, and men tied standing next to one another in three rows, like laundry, but the ropes were one above the other. These were the unbelievers, not good Muslims. They moved with the wind like laundry and a naked woman with a piece of rope around her neck was dancing before them [to torture them]. Then we returned to the Sheikh King's room and a rich vegetable meal was offered and a beautiful naked woman danced,

---

[55] He seemed like one of the Saudi royal family men.

playing with a garment that was offered to her. The Sheikh King said to me: 'This is what the good ones get. And now go home and come to see us again.' So I did and in a minute I was back at my barrack."

Salmân asked for my opinion as regards those things he described. My thoughts of his dream were as follows:

— What you saw confirms that you are in a state of conflict, an inner struggle occurs to you on being obligated to the tribal system, which commits you to your agnates, while your sympathy is given to the social setting in which you are left uncommitted, as a person. Not alone but to yourself. The dream seems to position you in disagreement with those who expect to see you begetting, thus to strengthen the tribe. Expectations as such uttered by your tribesmen distance you from them [because you are childless] and their embracing bond becomes a burden.

Your dream positions them as belonging to a primeval scene while on the other hand a Star War starts. It is a super modern event and, hence, forces you, the reluctant tribe's man, back into the embrace of your circle of agnates.

"Who do you [Gideon] think these tribal folks in this mountain hiding place are?"

— They sound like men in pain and at the same time seeming to enjoy or be taken to love the dancing women and the good food. They appear to like the luxurious event sharing a hearty meal. The entertaining scene distances them from traditional obligations. Doesn't it? This can feel like a conflict.

"And who is the one who activates the scene if not Allah, or who are those behind the shooting of fireworks, that appears like a show of a 'star war'?"

— Unlike the previous dream this scene doesn't show people. Both views are not a part of your previous experience but rather a one newly nourished by the media that now occupies your mind. It is surprising that vis-à-vis the inner split of your tribesmen, who are bound by an ancestral spirit, are proved to be in a non-tribal mood. The [agnatic] bond that commits you all to one another doesn't form the men into a coordinated, combatant unit, ready to unite and act for a common tribal cause. As an army the soldiers are not well prepared and therefore punished for the charge of unbelieving.

"Tell me precisely if there is something my dream indicates that I should do, and, if so, what is it? Do you think I have to do something after viewing these people? Who could they be for me?"

— Perhaps they were the elders of the Bedouin tribes, representing the Arabs in general. Who else could they be or stand for? There are only a few alternatives. Your dream shows you refer to them in a critical manner.

Pensively weighing how he should explain his predicament, Salmân preferred to tell me of another dream he had, a year earlier, i.e., before Summer 1967 and the last [Six Day] War.

3. c. Together with many soldiers and Moshe Dayan

"I find myself there together with many soldiers and [Moshe] Dayan among us, sitting on a slope of a high mountain near Jerusalem and looking at old houses on the mountain slope in front of us. Dayan placed his hand on my shoulder and said: 'Salmân, I shall try to fix these houses, stay here.' I answered: 'I shall be waiting here, you are the king.' So he went to the other mountain. Then I went home. I slept in the orchard alone and there came two giants. One, three and a half meters high, had a white beard and his shoulders, two meters wide. He told me to get up. The second of the two stood by the door and because of the strong light I couldn't see him. He shined like the sun. I said to him: 'I can't see you.' He then waved the palm of his hand before my eyes and I could see again. I asked him where he comes from and he said: 'from the 'Aqabah mountain.' He took out a little notebook and painted for me a door closing a cave, leading deep inside the mountain and said: 'I live here, my name is Mûsah [the Prophet, Moshe in Arabic]. Go tell Moshe Dayan that if he doesn't join the government they won't be able to win the war.'[56] They told me I am given a secret mission. What would you [Gideon] say about this?"

— Your dream indicates several problems you face: **a**. Those shining masculine giants occur to me as a reminder of another, maybe even biblical story of the Lord's Angel appearing in flame of the burning bush that is not consumed [Exodus 3; 2]. **b**. The precise location of the biblical Moshe's grave is unknown but it was somewhere in the Trans-Jordan mountains above the Dead Sea. Over there, all right, one peak is named after Mûsah. **c**. Your dream may indicate an attempt to merge the contrasting stories of the Arab and the Jew in agreement. As an Israeli Arab your life runs in between the two identities and you are shown in this dream trying to reach an accord that binds the two. **d**. In accordance with your dream Sidnâ Mûsa and Moshe Dayan keep on changing places. Isn't it so in your mind, an admiration for Dayan's charisma?

"He [Dayan] knows how to talk a direct language that I esteem."

— Moshe Dayan is elevated by your dream to be matched, equal to Sidnâ Mûsah, he is enhanced, perhaps higher than his

---

[56] Indeed, Moshe Dayan joined the government in the last days before June 5th, the day the war began.

actual position among the Israelis. Israel's success in the last war helped him regain this place at the Government table. He is back at the political top after a term in the shadows. Some feel displeased seeing him regain power while your dream says it is as it should be.

3. d. Giant Angels

"Will you listen here to another possibility of this dream: They [the giant Angels] said to me to tell Mûsi [an endearing nickname for Dayan] to allocate more room for patience [peace of mind], to allow a chance for peace made between the two peoples. He may suspect your mission. In this case we'll relate to you the stories of the three prophets: Mûsah, Issah [Jesus] and Muhammad. Then make a *shrâq* [flat bread] on the fire and split it into two; one half for him [Mûsah] and the other one eat yourself. Then more than one proof is needed, take my words, which he may half-heartedly accept, but be doubtful. Then tell him to put sheep and cows in one lee meadow ground to be fed and multiply, to be ready to feed mankind after the eighty years of trial. Tell that **only** to him, i.e., it must be a secret between the two of you. And indeed, Mûsah came to me one night, three months ago, and said; 'don't call me Moshe,' but I saw he was Dayan all right but in a *jinah* [paradise, here oasis] in a big desert place, and in the *jinah* trees and animals of all kinds and the gate is closing. I approached him saying: 'One is calling you,' and he answered: 'Then go tell him that I'm busy now. I have no one to give the key while I am away. Tell him that on giving the keys away I'll put my life in jeopardy.' What does it mean? Can you [Gideon] say something about my quandary?"

— The *jinah* [paradise] you saw has room for all the animals. It seems somewhat like Noah's Ark. Doesn't it? Only one substantial difference: Noah saved the species for themselves while your Mûsah saves mainly those edible ones as food for people, in order to save mankind after eighty years of a total war [Gog and Magog; Armageddon]. Isn't the fenced meadow here like a storage place for the survivors of the flood?"

> "I saw a black ship roaming in the skies followed by a fleet of black airplanes. I heard a big noise on the move up north. The color of the skies was red. Red like blood [Arabic and Hebrew - '*damm*']."

— Isn't it a threat of a terrible war that awaits us, a total war like a one that will engage us for many years to come? Shall people take your pronouncement seriously and get prepared either to prevent this war or have the means to get through it safely and win?

> "I saw the movement of many aircraft but it seemed that was not for a war-like clash. I felt like warning the people and Mûsah [Dayan] told me, in case the people won't take me seriously, heat an iron until it becomes red, for a *bish'ah*[57] test and be ready to touch it with your tongue. Don't be afraid, so they'll believe your words. And don't speak about it except with a religious man who will keep your words a secret between you two."

— Yes, yes, I am a Jew, though not a pious one and not a politician. I hear your dream and pay attention to your feelings and the trouble you see.

---

[57] A true-false test of touching (licking) heated metal by one's tongue. If burnt and bubbles appear it means a lying tongue. If it remains unharmed it means a person is telling the truth.

"Nor do I [a pious Muslim]. Take me for a one, I do not fast during the Ramadan month but for me this is not the important criterion of belief. A religious man is a trustworthy [*amîn*] one, meaning that he is known as one who is cautious [is frightened] of Allah as regards getting along with people."

— Are women included in your scheme of those you trust? Women appear in your dreams as those tempting the men you have in sight. You don't see them but sense that their beauty [attraction] does it. They lack personality or knowledge of the use of words. In fact of all those people you encounter it is only men with whom you are on speaking terms. Don't you dream hearing the voice of women too?

Salmân confirms that women too appear and speak in his visions but he cannot recall what they say. Or, he keeps their sayings to himself, out of any discussion.

Dream Teller 4. 'A. Salîm Recoils from Wrong Doing: A Warning that Comes in a Dream

'Ali Salîm (26), married and a father of three, resident of Shikun ha-Bedouin in Ramle, had been employed as a policeman for two years at the Be'er Sheva district. In the fall of 1968 he resigned the police service and began to work as a farming contractor, leading manual workers to fields and plantations. Born near Bîr Mishâsh (some 10 miles south of Be'er Sheva), his parents had followed him moving up north and after a time spent living in a tent, got a new house in one of the Bedouin quarters of Ramle. 'Ali summoned me to his yard to listen and help him understand "a disturbing dream" he has had repeatedly.

4. a. A scolding for misbehavior during an afternoon nap

"It [the dream] occurred to me first during an afternoon nap a few weeks ago and then again and also yesterday; I saw myself sitting naked outdoors, facing the street, my back turned to our home. Not even my underpants are on me. I dug a little pit for to sit, hiding, to remain unobserved by the folks passing by. Then suddenly filthy water started pouring out and into my pit, coming from home that makes me angry at my family. I pluck weeds and branches to be placed before my pit, to hide my nudity. I felt like urinating, meaning I must enter the restroom at our [his parents, eleven siblings and his nuclear family, wife and their children] home. At home all share four rooms and use one toilet, but I find out that all of a sudden the room's door has gone. No privacy for anyone there. My mother said to me: "Ali, don't you dare enter the [toilet] room! The water closet has sunk and beware you can fall down [to the cesspit].'

A brand-new [one year old] house and see, when I held the seat cover it remained in my hand [detached from the cover] and the water pipe broke, thus water covered the floor. What could I do? There was a little ditch that channels the water under the house. The sink in the kitchen was also broken and the water covered the floor. I felt like our home doesn't function any longer and I screamed for privacy."

— Being a work contractor don't you earn enough to allow your nuclear family an apartment of its own? I guess all would be grateful.

"Listen [disregarding my question] let me complete for you the telling. In another dream I was searching for the Quran, and an old Sheikh came and gave the Book to me, saying 'it is for you to read.' But no! The letters seem illegible, there were in fact no script-marks on them and, in addition, there were insect holes in the old copy of the holy Quran. The pages had an orange color and the letters were so pale. What do you think it means? Someone told me that in 'Ammân [the capital city of the Hashemite Kingdom of Jordan] a book, called *tafsîr el-ahlâm* [interpretation of dreams] may be found. How can we get it? What can you get out of such a dream? Or, did you hear about that book there?"

— I haven't seen or heard about this old book. We need to know who wrote it and where in 'Ammân we can look for it. Another question is why don't you move out of your parents' home? Get a different home to live in with your young family. The dream signifies quite clearly that your parents' place is overcrowded. Too many of you, your married brothers and your family members are grouped together and it is hard to live so and have peace of mind.

"Serving in the police provides 650 Lirot [then, about $270] a month, plus uniforms and some other fringe benefits you get. For operating a farming team [work contractor] I can get more than 1,200 Lirot a month. Forget about the clothing [uniform] and the day is longer and tiring. Neither one of the two salaries enable me buy a caravan [a nuclear family dwelling]."

— Then, invest some money and buy your home a new toilet seat. Repair the water pipe and teach your young siblings how to use it, keep it in order and clean enough.

"The trouble is that my father is about to get married again so he pushes my mother and her children [his brothers] to sleep all together in two rooms. My mother is sobbing because the *dhurrah* [co-wife] is about to come and make our home still more packed, but I can't tell my father what to do. His brothers put pressure on him to get married again [to begat more sons] and we have no right to speak."

— If your father has the money [6,000 Lirot bride price] needed to marry again, then sure enough he can afford a room or a caravan for his new bride, to be placed in the yard. Let your mother remain the mistress of her home. The Quran you saw in your dream signifies that it provides no solution for a situation like the one you face. This old Sheikh who gave you this Quran was a Sage who could read it aloud, in a meaningful way for you to follow, but alas, he didn't.

4. b. At our [tribal] shiq [Council of Elders] confronting admonishments of Sheikhs who swore me [to waste no time and beget children]

"I repeatedly see myself in dreams at our [tribal] Negev *shiq* where I sit confronting admonishments of Sheikhs who made me swear [in front of the men] to waste no time and beget children. Before Amîr [his elder son] was born [four years earlier], at the age of 18 I saw myself in a dream facing a trial of Sheikhs who forced me to travel away from home. Sitting among our tribesmen I was accused of wasting time that is needed to beget and enlarge our *qowm* [tribal group]. They pressed me to stay at home and see to the family growth. They didn't take my word that I feel too young for it, to fulfill the role of a father and work hard to feed my children,"

— The explanation above provided sense to the dream as it came to correct the dreamer, whose attitude made him evade a basic function of a married man. Thinking he was trying to forsake his crucial obligation as a tribesman to produce children, notwithstanding his young age, entangled him in an inner conflict. Weighed down by the tribes' elders he therefore appeared pressured, lest he wouldn't "mature" in the face of his responsibility as a young father.

A year later,[58] 'Ali Salîm called me to hear of the dream he happened to have some days earlier, in fact a night before his father's father passed away, when his family was still concerned about the condition of his health.

4. c. *Jiddi* [my Father's Father] on verge of dying

"*Jiddi* [my father's father] was in our home, very ill, on the verge of dying. In my dream I saw a gathering of many guests at our home [a sign of a funeral]. Many of them and us [his immediate family] among them began to dig holes in the ground, in the field nearby. They were seeding watermelon [work done in April]. To my surprise I saw some of the elders place a dead fish near every hole [mixed with the seeds]. I asked about it and what was explained to me I can't recall precisely. It was clear that the fish are rotten [*mjâyef, m'afen*]. A bad smell emanated from the family elders. One of the men stepped on a fish. Someone tried to stab a dead fish with a *shibriyya* [a dagger]. I helped him, took an ax and smashed the dead fish, disgusted. It made the field let off a terrible smell, a bad impression and, nevertheless, they still decided upon good manners, they behaved in accordance with comportment [*slûk*] typical of their

---

[58] August 22, 1969.

generation. It [the dream] makes me feel ridiculous and humiliated. What does it mean?"

—Your dream prepares you for a coming event, the death of your grandfather and the following days of mourning. It is a unique kind of experience that requires inner preparation. We all are to encounter this, in due time, in family events that require restraint and self-control. Although you know the tradition is not in your hands (it is in the hands of the tribe's elders), it determines what you are to do. You were perhaps in a position of being unaffected. You might have wished to distance yourself from here. But tradition commits you. Not only your fathers' generation. It commands your generation too. The bereavement implied in this dream may tell you to surrender to the family manner of mourning.

"Let's say you are right and I accept it, then tell me what am I supposed to do?"

— Your dream evinces a rejection of the elders' frame of mind. It tells you that their way of thinking cannot be overturned. You are to succumb. A suitable way out of this difficulty is for you to live in peace with them while embracing your modern perceptions for yourself. That is, don't hurt the feelings of your tribe's elders.

4. d. I see myself meeting Nâ'if my neighbor whom I respect and having no reason, I stab him three times in his stomach "Here let me tell you of another surprising dream I had [August 1969]. I sat together with friends in my home, and my neighbor Nâ'if who I respect most among them. All is friendly and then I see myself meet him [Nâ'if] on a Ramle street and having no reason that I can remember I draw my dagger and stab him three times in his stomach, once in his left hand and once his right foot. I recall it a hundred percent. Then I began to fear, how could I do this to him and he is a friend. Some five or six men of his family appeared and chased me running and calling me *khâ'in* [traitor] and I wake up in fear. Now tell me what is wrong with me to do such a thing? Can you?"

— What precisely does the presence of Nâ'if mean for you? Do you hold something against him? Or does he hold something against you?

4. e. When in love with the daughter of my Father's Brother "Listen please to another dream I had, about forbidden things. I see myself far away, in an unknown place. I left home because the company of my family members disturbed me. I can't breathe freely in their massive presence and I don't like them. The thing I saw while sleeping indeed happened and I think something real may come out of this dream. I'm there and in love with the daughter of my father's brother. In fact I dislike her. She tells me [in the dream] that she loves me: 'I constantly think about you,' and it all starts. Something begins to move between us but I leave this place [family dwelling and its girls]. I see myself and another boy plough the nearby field, riding the tractor. On coming home that evening and no family around other than this young girl I came inside her. Lying with her felt terrific for me, but she didn't move [had no satisfaction]. We were on our own as all the family members traveled to the Negev to mourn, as the custom is for the forty days [ritual conclusion of mourning] after the death of *jiddnâ* [our fathers' father]. In the dream we were alone at home. We were sure they [her family and mine] talk about us but, in fact, we find out in the dream that they didn't. We see *jiddnâ* [our mutual fathers' father] and understood from his face that from above he did not like the idea of us having sex."

— *Bint 'amm* marriage is traditionally supported, but, a. You are newly married and still very young. Probably the objection of your grandfather you face is for doing it [marrying a second time] too soon. b. In addition, you are not only too young but rather too poor to afford a second bride, feeding the second wife's children and going bankrupt. Between the positive and negative attitudes as regards your "new initiative" [towards your father's brother's teenage daughter] came to you in this dream of your deceased father's father.

Dream Teller 5. Salhah H.: Dreams Announcing a Yearning for Pregnancy

Salhah Abdallah (29) has been married to Hasan for ten years and they have no children. On Thursday midnight [when the Holy Friday enters] she dreamed and saw a group of Devils and Angels and among them a long bearded man who appeared to keep the peace between the bad and the good ones so as to relieve her of a headache. She felt ill, and taking a vow that if she were helped and the headache would vanish, she would make a sacrifice in Allah's name, thinking that that would help her conceive. Hasan, her husband, was the one to tell me about her dream, asking for my opinion. I was their guest. We (Salhah, Hasan and me) sat on their porch.

5. a. Devils and angels coming down from heaven to take note of her position and check her promise to give birth, to relieve her of her barrenness

"She saw *Shayâtîn* and *Malâyke* [Devils and Angels] coming down from heaven to take note of her position and check her promise [to give birth], to relieve her of her barrenness. Among them was one old man, who had a long white beard."

When she opened her eyes she told me [says Hasan] about it and the following day, Friday early morning, indeed, I slaughtered a lamb. To secure her pregnancy and take care of the health of her *dhurrah*'s [co-wife's] son, so to keep him away from Salhah's [envious barren co-wife] evil eye.

Hasan, Salhah's husband, asked me to reflect on what he told me (their concern) and join them for lunch.

— Amazed by the mix of Devils and Angels in a dream my question to Salhah, directed to her personally, that was what could she recall of these *shayâtîn* [Devils, pl. of *shîtân*] and of the *malâykeh* [pl. of *malak*]; how can we [in fact she] know the evil from the good ones in these circumstances? In other words, I asked if there are indications of the evil deeds of the first ones, vis-à-vis the good deeds of the second ones.

Salhah's answer:

> "They [the bad] were dark hence resembled me and my husband, but they had white garments on. They came from above though they had no wings. They gave no clear sign that they were sent by their king [Allah]. They just appeared at our home's door and you could see they were from out of this world. They didn't speak. But on seeing them I knew. So I made a promise that if they [Allah's messengers] would take away the curse of the headache, and give me back good health, I would donate a *harûf* [lamb] in their honor, to take along with them for Allah."

— All people can expect that Angels, once they appear together with Devils, will neutralize the impact of those bad ones. In accordance with your dream there seems to be a standoff in your favor. But the ancient Sage is there too, identifying and separating the two kinds of people [bad and good] then he can retain a good balance, that is, give a better chance in your favor for peace.

> "It's hard to judge people by the way they look. Often their appearance is misleading as regards their deeds. Those with bad intentions may look good and vice versa; an ugly looking person can turn out to be the one who does good."

— How about women in light of your experience? Are there women too among the Angels in this service of Allah?

> "Devils and Angels women [smiling]? If they exist I didn't hear about them. Perhaps Allah doesn't trust women for his missions, neither the good nor the evil ones. *Là* ! [No !] I often dream about my mother and her sisters, knowing that they could not be a part of anything bad that would happen to me, even be it in Allah's service [Allah against me]. I trust my women relatives, who are humble and loving, always thinking about and doing what is good for me."

According to Salhah, there are even gender barriers in determining women's fate for passively receiving good and evil. Men are the active transmitters of all that occurs. She therefore expects the announcement [of pregnancy] to be brought to her from Allah by male [Angel] messengers.

— On seeing two kinds of demons you instantly sense that they have arrived from an outer world. What was the indication you saw reading their faces? Reading faces [physiognomy] is meaningful. Could you distinguish the bad ones from the good ones, who of them decide the general objective of their joint presence?

> "Both exist for the mission of Allah that is nothing a do with their personal intents. Faces may hide desire. God's messengers I learned are presumed to reflect no desires or opinions of their own, so, only what they say or do counts. To prove what their mission actually was is meant to be seen afterwards [*post factum*], in light of what happens [once evil evaporates], when you can no longer see them."

Hasan, who followed me, asked that, and answers on behalf of his wife:

> "You can never know for sure [who God's messengers are] until your encounter with them is over. So it happened with Abunâ Ibrâhîm Al-Khalîl [our forefather Abraham of Hebron] who encountered Angels who looked like ordinary people, not knowing for sure who they really were."

— If so then we [simple people] must take into account a possibility that God has the will to test us; we slaughter a lamb for a seeming presence of Angels who may surprise us by being indeed Devils or vice versa?

May the divine messengers have "poker faces"? The idea seems strange. Salhah encountered dark individuals that could ease her attempt to read what their mission was, but her eyes were not able to discern what their real intent was. Reading their true mission from their facial expressions she left to be learned in months to come, once they were gone.

Dream Teller 6. Yunis: Dreams Come as an Aide Memoire

Ismâ'il Yunis (32), married and father of four, a contractor performing agro-machinery jobs, approached me asking to consult with him about to what extent the dreams that occur to us (to him) are controlled from above, i.e., by Allah. Based on what he heard from friends, it is Allah who plants dreams in people's minds, lest they forget what they should do. The way the question asked was, if dreams are designed from above (Heaven), why aren't they addressed in a direct manner, meaning in a straightforward way? To use an example that demonstrates what a "simple" dream can be the following dream story was brought to my knowledge:

6. a. An old Sheikh reminded me about a sum of money I placed aside, of which I had forgotten

"I saw in a dream an old Sheikh and he told me about a sum of money I had put aside, which I had forgotten and when recalled it was just where I had put it. In my dream I saw myself looking for it and I couldn't recall where I had hidden it. I did hide several amounts of money and most of them I did remember [where they were hidden]. Just this particular one I didn't. This dream reminded me precisely where I had hidden it, that I forgot for several years. It was under one *ballata* [a floor tile] in my home's yard. Just tell me how come for some years since I placed it there I couldn't recall precisely where it was, until this dream."

— Perhaps you placed the money inadvertently, being preoccupied with thinking of other things. It may also occur when we handle money we are not entitled to have. We may feel fear lest an unlawfully acquired sum that we hide may be discovered. Then it happens that we wipe out facts from our memory. Yet, it is in a niche, somewhere in our recollection, placed at the back of our mind, and can spring out in a moment of clarity or be brought back in a dream.

"What makes you think the money was not 'white' [legal]?"

— The question was why you forgot where you had placed it so I raised a possibility. You didn't tell me about the way you earned this sum but thought of the way you treated it; meaning, instead of investing the money in a way that would help it "grow" you left it hidden under a *ballata* for years.

"Is my seeing my deceased father's father in a dream and noting his comment reminding me where the money is implies that the money is legitimate now?"

— It is hard to answer that question. Tell me, if the dream had brought before you your deceased father's mother, would that have made any difference?

"Women can use the money for shopping but don't know a thing about the way the money is obtained [meaning negative; grandmother couldn't tell me where the money is]."

6. b. Khalifa [a Jewish colleague] evinces a fatal dream that had happened to his family in Libya

"You say not a legitimate source of income [harsh reaction] acts to makes us 'forget' about it. You remind me of a story I heard from a Jew about the Jews in Libya [not only Arabs handle 'black' money]. Khalifa told me of something that had happened to people [Jews] he knew in Libya.

A Jew got stuck outside of town when Sabbath eve was drawing near. At that moment he had a big sum of money in his pocket [on Shabbat the keeping of money in one's pocket is prohibited by laws of the Torah]. On his way, on the outskirts of town was a Muslim cemetery so he placed the money there, at the head of a grave. He kept on walking home and thought: —'On Saturday night right after sunset, I shall return here and fetch my money.'

However, it was the grave of an old Arab and he appeared in his offspring's dream and told him about the money. His son thought: '*Wallahi*! [by God], my grandfather is dead now for forty years. It can't be true.' But his grandfather came to him again that night and shook him out of bed. He then got up, took the hoe and went right to the cemetery. There he dug at the place of his grandfather's head and found the money. Of course, he took it and went home.

On the conclusion of the Sabbath the Jew returned to the Muslim cemetery and didn't find his money. He had to relate the story to people and ask them if they saw someone sneaking in - -. At that time in Libya there was more trust in 'giving a word' of honor. Unlike the lack of trust between people these days, words were more seriously taken then than now. For a person to take something away and say: — 'I didn't see it' was more difficult during olden times. So the son of the dead man told the Jew about his grandfather's appearance in his dream, and eventually gave him his money back. What the Jew had learned from this experience is written in the Torah: — 'An Arab is not to be trusted even after forty years in the grave.'"

— To the best of my command of the biblical text, there isn't such a verse as that. Rather, my understanding of your dream is that it made you angry. Isn't that correct?

> "Tell me, don't you believe that some people have the ability to effect the dreams of other people? So to shape them [dreams] the way they please? Say, some people would like you to see the nature of things through their eyes."

— We can pray to make those we love have good dreams of us, thus make them love us. Or wish for those we hate to dream of us in a bewildering manner, to be bothered by dreadful dreams about us, hence teach them a lesson. But how can we verify the effect of attempts to plant a dream in someone's mind? This is beyond our reach. Not possible.

> "For sure, and it was clear to the Arab and the Jew, it is that Allah stands on the side of the Arab [raising the history of Jews in the lands of Islam]. The Jews must rely on the mercies of good-hearted Arabs. Isn't that true? On leaving them [Jews] all by themselves, who will guarantee their lives? Who'll defend them?"

— On treating the Jewish communities of Arabia, the Prophet Muhammad was not compassionate. See what was done to the Bani Qurayzah and the inhabitants of the Khaybar, two communities that were robbed and then exterminated. They were farmers, herders, artisans and traders living in the Arabian Peninsula for centuries, and most of them perished under Muhammad 'Abdallah (the Prophet) and his followers.[59]

---

[59] See Kressel in Paul Hare & Kressel (2001), Part 3. Chapter 12.

"Because of what they [the Khaybar Jews] did; they behaved like that Jew [in the dream above] who dared place money on Friday Eve in a Muslim cemetery."

— Your idea resembles the idea Mr. Khalifa had; he, a Jew, doubted the honesty of Muslims. For this he made use of a story of a person who saw his long-deceased father's father in a dream, to incriminate the totality of the Jewish people. Attempts to decipher dreams by means of a folktale, even if understandable, are often false. We shouldn't try to analyze the construction of a dream story in order get at a divine pronouncement.

Dream Teller 7: Sâber: Dreams are a Reflection of Traditional Legends

Ibrâhîm Sâber, 38 years old, a resident of the Jawârish neighborhood of Ramle and a factory worker, father of seven,[60] asked me to listen to a disturbing dream that had occurred to him the day before yesterday.

7.a. "Preparing for this day ['Id al-Adhah holiday], a day before yesterday, on my way home I passed through the town's market. There I bought a goat. We are commanded to slaughter a goat [rather than a lamb] on behalf of our children, this day, a tradition we inherited from our fathers who came from Libya.[61] Last night I dreamed that I was about to kill my elder son. Having a knife in my hand I approached him but seeing the old Sheikh of our tribe standing in my way I awoke from this dream in great fear; how could

---

[60] February 1970, the time of the Sacrifice Holiday [*'Id al-Adhah*].

[61] The Jawârish communities cherish traditions brought over from their land of origin, Libya. See Kressel (1974).

I dare think such a thing? Just thinking of harming my beloved firstborn son makes me tremble. Allah, no doubt, had put this dream in my head. Or how would you [Gideon] explain it? It was shocking so I told it to friends. To my amazement also Ghazi Abu Sêif [a neighbor and an age mate], to whom I told this dream, related to me that he too had had precisely the same dream, as regards his dearest son. An old, white bearded Sheikh of theirs [forefather of the Abu Sêif lineage] saved the life of his dearest son from his own knife."

— Much has been discussed about this holiday on all Middle Eastern radio stations that broadcast in preparation for the *'Id al-Adhah* to come. The idea of sacrificing a lamb to replace the sacrifice of a child is penetrating people's minds.

"Who would ever ponder killing one of his sons in Allah's name? Tell me. Do you believe it could have ever crossed people's mind, and could it be translated into real practice?"

— It seems it was. There are accounts of this tradition in ancient texts, including the Bible and the Quran. To keep one's beloved family intact, to protect your herds, the custom was to sacrifice one of your dearest offspring to God. A lamb hence was taken to replace human sacrifice, to please the voracious Allah. Our ancestors did such things out of fear. One does it in God's honor, in the hope that God in return will take care of the rest of our loved ones. Giving God the dearest one of yours for his blessing supposes security for all the others.

"So it was an ancient [*jâhelli*=pre-Islamic] custom. No wonder the elders [*shuyûkh*] decided to stop it. I spoke about my dream with Sheikh 'Amer [the highest tribal authority] and he told me that men are **supposed** to have such dreams to teach them. 'It is a good sign you have had it!' So, in order to feel compassion for their children God shows them their father in a dream. [Allah] put them in a position of harming their dearest by reminding them how they were pardoned. Fathers are prevented from doing it [slaughtering their children], each one by his elders. If so, probably, our ancestors came to tell our own fathers to keep us alive."

Dream Teller 8: J. Hmeda: Dreams Call for Decorum

Jubrîn Hmeda (45), a father of eight, owner of the local grocery store. On May 1st 1970 that occurred that year together with the day to pay a visit [*zyâra*] to the grave of *Nâbi Sâleh*, I happened to pass by the cemetery nearby and met Jubrîn seated on the grave mound of his father's brother Yussef praying. On ending his prayer Jubrîn saw me and called me to approach him, where he said:

8. a. A goat for a sacrifice – Holiday brings dream as though I am about to kill my elder son

"See me here, last night I dreamed about *'ammi* [his father's brother] Yussef. He summoned me in the dream to visit his graveside and so to oblige him, I came. Allah made me dream about *'ammi* [who died some 15 years earlier]. Exactly last night, knowing that it is the day of *Nâbi Sâleh* whose grave is here [by the urban cemetery] and knowing myself and my plans intending to do other things this day. The dream came to correct me and make me come here — despite my plans. I was told [by him] to honor his grave and that brought me here. After my father died *'ammi* took care of me, looked after my mother and me."

Jubrîn was a month old when his father died. He grew up under the patronage of his father's brother [*'amm*] Sheikh Yussef.

— It was your *'amm*'s request that made you come here today. Were there [in this dream] any other elements that you were commanded to do on visiting the grave?

8. b. "You are to come to visit me!" To honor the grave of my Father's Brother

"I cannot recall from the dream precisely what else was in it other than the instruction: — 'You are to come to visit me!' Meaning to honor *'ammi* Yussef and his wife Mariam today was to visit the grave. I am seated on the mound in order to let him feel me: I'm here! Was it that Allah had in mind to ask me to fulfill additional missions? No doubt I'd have to follow whatever he said. Allah could request of me to do everything. If he [Allah] wanted me to do more, why didn't he tell me?! What else do you [Gideon] think he could have requested of me to do today?"

— Naturally the preparations for "The Day of *Nâbi Sâleh*" made people hear and think about him. Thus true believers among them, as yourself, were especially affected. It could be that the words heard during the last days have made many people dream about the *Nâbi*.

"Not exactly so. *'Ammi* [my father's brother] in this dream made me aware of the forgotten fact that we are after all created to die. Since we tend to remember what commits us to do tomorrow [one step forward], the facts of life [and death] that come to us whether we like it or not, our dreams come as a reminder of the *'âlam el khulûd* [the world of eternity]."

Dream Teller 9: 'A. er-Rahmân: Dreams Comes to Make You Face Reality, Help Us See the Way Things Really Are.

'Abd er-Rahmân (32), an agricultural worker, descendant of an Egyptian farmer (*fallâh*), was a tenant at will of the Abu Sân'e tribe (Bedouin of the Be'er Sheva district). Married to two women, a father of eight children, he invited me to attend the feast in honor of the circumcision of three of his sons.[62] Sitting at my side he related to me the details of a dream he had, not long ago, and asked for my opinion of what it meant: -

9. a On the way to visit my *bint 'ammi* [Father's Brother's daughter] along with her dead Father, his paternal Uncle

"We [a family group] went to visit *bint 'ammi* [my father's brother's daughter]. Her deceased father drove the car. The two of us are not on good speaking terms. Since the day she married a stranger [not a paternal cousin], anger prevails between us. In my dream I join him [his old father's brother] though he passed away a very old man, some years ago. Now he appeared before me wearing a long white *thowb* [robe]. He asked me to get in his car and go, and he was speaking as he drove to where she [his daughter] lives [in her husband's family's place]. On arriving I didn't feel well. I was not up to talking with her [because of the old anger that she did not marry him]. I said to him [her father] that I am thirsty. She heard me say it and

---

[62] May 1970, on the outskirts of the Jawârish neighborhood.

brought me a rusty tin box full of water. But in order not to offend her I drank it all [although it was filthy], as if it were an ordeal put before me, and the water wet my cheeks and shirt.

Then we returned to his car and drove on to a nearby Bedouin campsite, to take part in our relatives' celebration. Many people were there, all in white robes as in the gathering of the *hujâj* returning from Mecca [where all are in white],[63] but I felt displeased and didn't feel like seeing them and, all the more so, to talk to any one of them. Can you [Gideon] say what it all means to me?"

— It seems pretty simple. The anger between you and *'ummumak* [your father's brothers and, in fact, all your elder agnates], who hurt you by not letting you marry your *bint 'amm*, still troubles your mind. Isn't it simple? This dream comes to tell you that despite your conscious position [anger], there is no sense in holding this grudge. By holding onto it you lose more. In this case speaking terms in the family circle are more important than you choking down your wrath. The dream tells you to make up with them, to improve your position among them because it is better for you.

9. b. A fed up, nervous reaction towards a paternal Grandmother that brought about her death

"Because of them [his old agnates = *'ummum*] I left their campsites and came to live in the north. So [a long pause], Saturday night [yesterday] I had another dream: — I am nervous, sit at home and my grandmother, or was it my wife, it was hard to recall

---

[63] Wearing white robes stands for wearing shrouds, ready to be buried.

which one of them it was, sits before me and makes me still more nervous, on preaching to me respect for my elders. Just nonsense. Right between me and her were cups of tea. I kick them towards her. A cup hits her, breaks and cuts her big toe. Her blood pours out as if I had slaughtered her; I see that she became like a sacrificed sheep. I had killed her. And the big commotion explaining myself starts all over again."

— The elder women of the family are displeased at your attitude to the elder men of the family. They judge you critically because of your childish behavior, isn't that it? And you are impatient with them. Your bride was picked for you despite your wishes and, then, on your own, you found a second wife, so now all respect you more.

9. c. [Similar to the above] A fed up, nervous reaction towards a paternal Uncle causes his death

"It's not just a matter of the women's attitude, not only them. Here listen, I had as well this dream: I caught one old man who resembles one of my *'ummum* by his neck and strangled him though I had no desire to kill, but I caused his death. Shocked by the thing I did I am bothered by the fact that I don't know exactly who this person was."

— See, time and again your dreams warn you of the results of blind anger; it can cause you to commit a horrible crime and, in fact, perhaps in vain. Your dream leaves you uncertain, who will be your next victim, if he deserves your punishment or not.

"Doing this I think now perhaps he was *ibn 'ammi* [my father's brother's son] who should have married her [my wife]. But he went to Gaza as if for a day's visit then indeed went to Brazil. A month later someone came to give us his regards, and out of anger I strangled him [this messenger or better perhaps the absconding *ibn 'ammi*]. Same as I broke the cup [in the previous dream] is what I did to him [revenge = kill him]: *'Sâl ed-dâm farj el-hâm'* = the spilling of blood relaxes [your] inner unrest."

— But it entangles your feelings in rage towards the rest of your family. And not less, mind the complexity with the law; the police may come to find you if you don't control your temper.

'Abd er-Rahmân was forced to take for a wife another cousin, despite his love for her younger sister, who was given to someone else.[64] Troubling his mind, asking why his desire was not met, 'Abd er-Rahmân's attitude could not justify his family's matchmaking policy. When this occurred, some ten years earlier, domestic disputes came about and were never resolved, frustrating him, and making him feel as if he had been abandoned. Close-fisted, dreaming of an act of revenge 'Abd er-Rahmân related a dream he had to an elder person belonging to another tribe. This man taught him to understand the following:

"On seeing bleeding flesh [an injury] or a bleeding person in a dream it is a bad omen. Expect that something very bad will happen to you the following day. Beware! Stay at home! Don't go to work!

On seeing in a dream a good meal, well-cooked food and cold water being offered to you, note that it is a

---

[64] To an extent, this is similar to the story of the biblical Jacob and the daughters of Laban, Leah and Rachel.

good omen. Expect that good things will happen to you along the way, this day.

As well, on seeing yourself floating, like in a boat on still water, then calm down. Expect to meet good things as you sail along during the day.

If in your dream you are forsaken, left behind like when the bus you have been waiting for doesn't stop or has left the station and you didn't make it, then go back! If you had in mind to start a new job, then forget about it! When thoughts of a partnership with someone are on your mind, then they must be forsaken! You have had in mind to get married? Drop it! Think of another bride! Start anew! Knowledgeable people have taught me about a book to be found in the markets of 'Amman, Jordan, called *'Ilm en-Nafs* [the study of soul] which when I read it I will understand all I need.

In case you meet an elder Sheikh of yours [forefather] lower your eyes. You have no chance to change your position, you must be reconciled with whatever you've got.

9. d. Immoral abuse of an unknown hired woman caused anger above

"My neighbor Hussein and I joined forces as contractors, employing farm hands, workers [mainly women] we brought from West Bank villages to fields. We were growing vegetables together then shared the profit between us. In my dream I saw the two of us in a jeep, riding in a ravine [*wâdi*], in a desert land, and with us an unknown woman. He [Hussein] took the wheel and she sat next to him, between us. I sat by the other window, relaxed. He drove on a field road rather slowly and my foot touched the spare tire of the right front wheel. Then suddenly he began to speed up, jumped forward. I fell out and she [the woman worker from the West Bank] closed the door behind me as they drove away. I try to hold on to the back door but missed it. An old bearded Sheikh was there and saw it. He called it *zinâ* [fornication]. The following day, remembering that dream and the clue the interpreter gave me, I broke the agreement with him and didn't join him for work. He was surprised and came to speak so nicely to me, and I then reconsidered my withdrawal and joined him again.

The following week we were back at work together. Being illegal employers [contractors], we went to fetch [illegally i.e., not via the Employment Service] workers from the West Bank. The trouble was that, that time we were caught and fined IL750. Figure it out, of the return we got for three months of work each of us took only IL185. Had I listened to my dream and quit the contact with Hussein, I could have saved paying the fine and ended up with IL468 [more than half the fine amount of IL750]. If you see what I mean, the dream spoke truth! Had I followed my dream's message and obeyed what it said, I could have been now better off. I told my dream to Sâlmah, a spinster living nearby, aged 42, who knew how to tell people's fortunes = *al-baht*, who listened to dreams.

She heard my dream story and more facts as regards that woman in Hussein's car, and interpreted the meaning of the complication I faced as follows:

9. e. Sâlmah: A Clever Woman Interprets 'Abd er-Rahmân's Dream Story

"Once women, **not** in capacity of a mother, sister or wife, appear in men's dreams they stand there answerable only to the whims of men. They [women] cannot be charged as guilty for arousing these men. There [in men's dreams], women succumb to manly conditions [*hasab az-zurûf*], i.e., they are expected to have no say as regards rude facts of life or anything of worldly affairs. Their presence in men's dreams is largely passive. They react to the expectations revealed to them without any direct or indirect intervention. Women stand still and shun intervention for a lack of initiative [*mubâdara*] on their behalf. They passively await the initiative suddenly revealed and addressed to them, hoping to bypass it unharmed. Their being always at risk is similar to the way breadwinning is for men. In dreams the daughter is like the world ['*fi al-ahlâm al-binet zay ad-dunyâ*], meaning, she is there, passive, having no desires of her own. To begin with, your position [talking to 'Abd er-Rahmân] arguing with your partner has no chance. He is moved by his whims."

'Abd er-Rahmân finished quoting **Sâlmah,** then elaborated adding a description of the impact of her words when addressed by him to their workers, during breakfast, as follows:

"The women [the other workers] heard me tell about Sâlmah's interpretation of Hussein's behavior and broke into laughter [i.e., the talk went on during a breakfast break, was followed by a few of them], which in fact came true. I was caught [by the police] driving the [illegal] workers' car and he [Hussein] went on unharmed. What can you [Gideon] say about it?"

131

— Your dream comes to make you cautious about your partner who drags you into places where you don't feel like being. It tells you, 'better mind your own business.' Your ancestor Sheikh appears to negate this fornication which you don't like either. The dream tells you that had you obeyed your inner logic and not succumbed to your fornicating neighbor-partner — this dream could have been unnecessary, i.e., avoided.

Dream Teller 10: Dreams Help Hold the Tribal Spirit Strong [i.e., Agnatic Ties Well Nourished] by Dreams That Verify Inner Kinship Truths

Hamdân esh-Shamâli (32), a professional mason and a secondary contractor for construction works, a descendent of immigrants from Egypt and a father of four, told me his nightmare, dreams of obligations to his tribesmen. A position of dependence, meaning a need to leave home in search of refuge in the Negev [his previous camp site] once "a hot headed agnate, a distant, 'doubtful' [*mashquq, mush wâdeh*] relative entangled us all in an exchange of blows. Belonging to a tribe gives rise to doubts that come in dreams, that awaken questions about who is a real kin, who is less real and who is not kin.

10. a. When agnatic ties are on trial

"A careless *qarîb* [agnate] can entangle you despite your will and drag you unwilling into a fight with people you have no reason to hate. After he [the dispute-causing *qarîb*] did what he did we were reluctant to leave our homes [go on *tîba*[65]] together with them [distant relatives who kindled the feud], all because of him, who started it all. We accused him of what he did

---

[65] Leave home to escape retaliation and therefore find refuge in the hospitality of a dignified (powerful) Sheikh.

on behalf of our paternal ancestors. We were praying that our *Shuyûkh* would move in, expecting them to teach him and his immediate family group, and thus cause them to behave themselves."

The spirits of the ancestors in their divine space were approached through prayer to mobilize the deceased paternal forefathers to appear in their full authority before the troublemaking group, in dreams, and demand of them to hold down their criminal sons. Along with regular religious prayer, beginning with 'Al Fâtiha', before addressing a request to the Divine, the tribal Sheikhs are approached in prayer that they should have their say in Allah's court as a guarantee to get the desired result.

10. b. Hamdân's version of paternal ancestors affecting their descendants' dreams

"*Jdûdnâ 'alamûnâ* [our paternal ancestors taught us] that each of us needs to feel responsible for the group's unity. Somewhere in Egypt's desert, it is told a deep well is to be found. On the walls of this well are written the names of all the [Arab] families living on the earth. I saw myself in a dream going down the *Bîr al-anfâs* in search of my family's origins. All names that are to be found there are engraved on the walls, to enable interested people to embrace their relatives' souls while they hover above the round walls and find out who their paternal ancestors were. In my dream I had to find out for sure what our legal position is because of our [feud] situation. But there I had to peer because of the dim light and the tiny letters of the writings, so I was disappointed and I got out of it [the deep well], scared of the responsibility to decide for myself, who are our real paternal relatives, and hence who should be expected to stand by our side, fighting the stupid new feud. Do you believe such a well exists? Or, how can we possibly discover what we are to do? What would you [Gideon] examine if you were in my position of facing the fate of our lineage and the *Bîr al-anfâs* walls?"

— Even if we doubt the existence of this *Bîr al-anfâs,* it is an interesting, beautiful legend. Suppose it is hidden somewhere in the desert and an Angel is on guard there, hovering above while a second Angel is busy writing new names on the walls of this dark, bottomless well. He must move himself there flying around like a bat, with a toolkit of instruments to hew that huge number of names. And how can he be informed about every birth of a child in such a vast area, for that immense number of years? Your dream indicates you realize that the well cannot be more than a very fine legend, meaning that, regrettably, your question cannot be answered.

Dream Teller 11: Dreams Come to Encourage, Let Us Have Hope and Trust in Our Future

Ta'ilah (65), the elder wife of the Jawârish Sheikh 'Amer, mother of eight, spoke about dreams with 'Aishah (38), one of her daughters, and told her about her mother ('Aishah's maternal grandmother) and the way she understood dreams. They were sitting peeling vegetables for supper together, discussing Ta'ilah's late mother. I heard aboutTa'ilah's words spoken to her daughter while visiting her home. I learned from her another facet related to dreams, a unique traditional approach to accepting and interpreting dreams.[66]

---

[66] In February 1972, I got a note about the talk from her daughter, i.e., a second hand interpretation based on what her mother had said.

11. a. Ta'ilah and her Mother's View of Dreams

"For my mother dreams occur to us sent from God [*min Allah*]. Such are especially those dreams that come to us following cases of difficult, i.e., shocking experience. Then we [people] face a divine message sent to encourage us, we learn who supports us. The appearance of our forefathers in dreams is a sign of Allah speaking. They are his emissaries."

— Often dreams are not benevolent but rather revealing, often they are unpleasant, even traumatic.

"She [her mother] knew about it, of course, and related to bad dreams as an indication brought to our attention that our situation is after all fine and we shouldn't spoil it by doing wrong things. Thanks to this view of hers, her clientele [largely women] come to see even negative occurrences in their life in an encouraging way, thus justifying the positive side of what was happening and putting things in a supportive light. My mother listened to dreams people told her and she understood that they are given to us to strengthen the heart. It was her practice to mainly listen and to say little, but by what she said you understood that [as in modern psychoanalysis] you are better off whatever the experience, after having the dream you had. Her message always showed the dreamer that Allah is on her side, concerned with all that happens because that is his place to keep evil away from us. Dreams evince that someone is above to secure his *'abed* ['slave,' here a follower, a disciple] a safe future. Ordeals come to strengthen us and help us endure hardship. Ancestors [men, the tribe's founders] carry encouragement to their progeny."

— In accordance with my experience dreams can carry meanings of a wide variety of things; some bring up substantial messages while some reflect very little, even a meaningless collection of nonsense that cannot tell much. For sure not the simple message saying: "put your trust in Allah."

> "The dreams are planted in us to confirm that he [Allah] sees the hardships we [dreamers] go through. Meaning that a reward for the hardship we encounter will follow soon."

— Divine promises, foretelling a better future, occur in dreams as well as warnings about bad things about to happen, e.g., if we do not stop behaving wrongly, or change direction.

> "People on a daily walk through life do not always feel they are being led astray. Then Allah shows them [by means of dreams] the better way to proceed and how to improve themselves."

According to Ta'ilah's understanding, dreams are planted in people's minds like doses of divine medicine, to help them, on condition that they use them properly. Properly means to take the corrections shown to them in a way that gets them through predicaments. Listening to her, dreams encourage the dreaming [women] to accept all that comes in life that is Allah's personal will. Obstinate positions can make our minds rigid, disregarding the correction the dream shows.

11. b. Search for a Dream and be Sincere! It Will Come

Dreams are given and with them are guarantees for future, desired events. Nâjlah, twenty-two years old, daughter of formerly nomadic Bedouin parents, matriculated, a poet, matched in marriage to an illiterate man, expecting her first child in a month, tells me of warnings directed to her by the elder women of her husband's family, particularly now when her day of delivery comes closer.[67]

Dream Teller 12: Nâjlah's Doubting Comment: Faith and Skepticism

The dynamic of the former Bedouin belief reflects a balance between faith and skepticism, the empirical and mystical causes.

12. a. Inculcating women's lore to encourage a dream in which one's paternal elders appear

"They arrived at our home, my mother-in-law and a few of her age-mates [elderly paternal of the *'ummûm* women], enter and sat themselves down for a talk. They came to ask me to shun association with women while they are menstruating ['*âda esh-shahârriya*] lest they will, innocently or on-purpose, harm my chances to conceive again.

I asked them [cynically] if I am to inquire of every visiting young women, who of them dares to approach me while menstruating? They heard me and understood my cynical criticism. Sâbrah said: Before I delivered Jum'a [her three year old first born son] to my surprise, *jideti* ['*ammah*', her father's mother] appeared in my dream saying: 'Take care to avoid meeting Jme'ah [second paternal cousin who had not conceived after three years of marriage], because if she menstruates she will prevent your conceiving a second child. To secure success in giving birth, in such a case,

---

you'll have to ask her to give you some drops of her menstrual blood, which you'll have to mix with water and then take the mixture for washing the top of your head. On releasing your chance to conceive, she can still have an effect on your likelihood to keep it [lest miscarriage occur] then cause you a uterus closure, and then, she'll be apt to refuse to help, leaving you barren. Did you see Sheikh 'Aâdel in one of your dreams?"

Sheikh 'Aâdel died in old age, some twenty and more years earlier. His appearance in dreams was taken as a promise of divine protection, provision of immunity, to secure the woman's luck, that is a good chance to conceive again, after the delivery of her child, with no trouble. Nâjlah did not meet the old ancestor in any of her dreams and was instructed to think much about him and therefore summon him to her dream: "To secure a good dream, think of your elder and help him come to you."

— Dressed as in a dream, your husband's paternal aunt (*'ammah*) could have warned you and guided your behavior by virtue of a belief (superstition) that took hold of her mind as well as the minds of her unaware women's circle. Provided that Allah speaks to us through our dreams, or that Allah plants night dreams to affect our comportment, it can be used to promote warning. As a matter of fact, such dreams may come directly to us, as, e.g., by your in-law circle of women. Could not it be so?

"Can it be that magical processes begin in women's minds by means of planted dreams? My in-law women told me of a woman who lost her pregnancy through miscarriage at six months. Then she gave birth to two girls [could not conceive another son]. It all happened after a *ghula* [female Demon] desired her son for herself. She appeared in her dream at the sixth month of her pregnancy to snatch it from her. The *ghula* then told her that she'd lose the son in her favor and so it happened."

— It seems that an initial fear that something is wrong with her fetus caused the dream about the hostile *ghula*. Not the other way around.

"They [her elder in-law women] say that Allah warns the Muslim women in their dreams, by means of the tribe's paternal elders, to cover their heads and arms fully [when outside the home]. But because of those who disregard Allah's messages and walk around with their arms uncovered, Allah strikes us with *jafâf* [drought] this year."

Nâjlah related to me the dream she expected to have, that did not come. It had been suggested for her to see while asleep an old paternal elder (not a particular person) of her husband's father's lineage. Just a dignified Sheikh to gain a sign she has him to protect her and secure her fertility potential in the service of her husband's tribe.

"My question to her was why is it that an image of a male elder should necessarily stand on the side of good. How about the feasibility of a negative dream, showing a bad experience a woman can have with her husband's elders. I asked if it might have happened in her dream that she sees an old trickster that colors, of necessity, her view of him and his like in black. I asked how come the image of old men, who are not always an ideal but often tough, are to be taken as a good omen?"

— Yes, and in addition to your question, why just elderly men (and not, e.g., a dignified grandmothers) stand there on the side of good order and dignity?

Nâjlah, a sensible person, thought about my words but found no answer to my question. *"Al malâyke kulhom min al dhukûr"* [all Angels are male]. It is most likely a cultural notion, created to direct people's thoughts and guide them to expect revelations from elderly men in dreams or substantiate just this kind of vision in which men take on the role of God's messengers.

— Did you ever see an elderly grandmother in a dream, a grandma who appears in the capacity of a messenger asking you to maintain or amend your manners? Do maternal figures correct you or redirect your behavior nowadays, in varying modes of living? Do the circumstances allow it? An experienced grandmother, possessing the knowledge of the ancient generations of women, can call to the next generation of women to provide them with good advice, caring for their great granddaughters.

> "[Smiling] I must admit, no one like my mother and her sisters, or my mother-in-law ever mentioned the appearance of women in dreams. I guess people do have dreams showing them their grandmothers, them too, but a grandmother's visit doesn't bear the same significance as the visit of a grandpa can have. His appearance in a dream is what all are waiting for, more often than not at times of lunar eclipse."

On noting Nâjlah's comments and agreeing with them I concluded (1976) this part of my study. Although always attentive to the telling of dreams, I did not give it much of my time. Among the Negev Bedouin I was not as patient a listener to dream stories as I was among Bedouin in Ramle. People told me of dream images they had over the last decades and, in fact, they largely revealed the same pattern I had noted in town. This kind of dream telling appears as a miraculous experience more than an indication of a personal or psychological problem, a happening that confirms the dreamer's relatedness to his tribal core more than an inner event that calls for attention to details, often a clinical use of dream material, probing her/his state of mind.

V. Concluding Remarks

Millennia old traditions that were culturally shaped from the time thought of as the dawn of civilization retain their hold and affect the perceptions we have and transmit to our coming generations. Ancient patterns of thought still affect our ways of thinking as in dreaming. This study portrays both yearning for particular kinds of dream and doubts of the real significance of our dream material, be it as a measure by which to amend our behavior or a nonsensical echo of events we have experienced.

The various attitudes seen in dreams mentioned above include a lasting belief that some dreams carry out Allah's wishes for us, his followers, human beings. The benefit of this conviction is used to urge people (not necessarily by frightening them), to rectify their obligations to Allah. In other words, persuade the public to obey the imperatives of their creed. When this view of dreams is expressed time and again skeptics need to be careful and silence their doubts. Welcomed dreams are those that suit an ideal model, mostly those that sound enlightening or prophetic. Often dreams, after being told in public, are revered as carrying a word of Allah or a reminder of his existence to the forgetful. They evoke awe and gain much attention. But rarely do dreams stand categorically as sacred expressions. On the other hand, now and then a dream sounds trivial and is seemingly vain, a mere foolishness and a waste of time. It happens that dreams may be deceitful. Or dreams may be pure pitiful vanity (Kantrowitz, 2001).

"The dreaming is many things in one. Among them, a kind of narrative of things that once happened; a kind of charter of things that still happen; and a kind of *logos* or principle of order transcending everything significant for aboriginal man" (Stanner, 1956). But along with the transition of illiterate societies reaching modernity, their culture evolves and reshapes the images in dreams they expect to have.

Any understanding of disguised instructions in dreams that wait to be understood and followed by us due to their carrying divine judgments has a universal foundation. Receiving God's directions, his guidelines, through dreams is a ubiquitous idea. People's expectation is to find comfort in dreams, the "products of sleep" that are often presented as a riddle to be solved. This belief is shared in folklore worldwide. The Divine addresses such solutions that mortals are in need of, but in a disguised form. Largely speaking his style is to disguise the messages he sends, or leaves them covered up, to be uncovered, naturally, by those people who feel engaged, and to make it clear that it is up to them to decipher his pronouncements — or not, as they please.

Though dream expressions may include important messages, they can get lost notwithstanding the enlightening truth in them, which is then apt to be forgotten. We cannot fail to acknowledge the fact that to decipher those secrets concealed in our dreams remains optional; inattention to whatever dreams bring occurs to us regularly, and not heeding dreams that appear dangerous means that serious but meaningful ones get lost too. In case they contain new guidelines of importance for us all dreams require much attention, even dreams that express vanity and do not seem to deserve a second look. Attention to both these possible versions necessitates careful deliberation from us as individuals. Important too is the group to which we ascribe, that pays better attention to what happens during our nightly sleep. Traditional analysts who are often the guiding elders of the group are the ones who decide whether a dream is "decent" or "false" which is in essence not a simple judgment, not a simple task (Khan, 1972; Shulman & Sroumsa, 1999).

The search for what is meant by what appears to us at night is ancient. Primeval examination of dreams has posited this problem since time immemorial. Ancient cultures handled this problem in a way that resembles the way this dilemma is posited before us now and in much a similar way.

Turning a dream over and over again in search of its meaning and possible implications (Quinodoz, 1999) does not differ in the Bedouin neighborhoods of Ramle and the conventional modern understanding of dreams when compared to what it was in ancient societies. The distinction here is regarding dreams as saying things of importance for the future of the tribe as a whole. A suggestion of an action that would compel the dreamer alone is common in psychoanalysis, but for him to be included within his entire group transcends the individual, imagining that person can stand "outside" or "away from" him or herself. Such situations correspond with the ability to regard eventualities that have occurred or are about to occur, awaiting our judgment. No wonder thoughts may influence one's dream wishes.

According to Khamisah (above), once former Bedouin settle in towns they come to resemble their immediate neighbors, individuals who were brought up in other surroundings. Most people share the ability to note dreams of greater importance. Variety in the quality of dreams is common and clear to all. Certainly all notice the importance of dreams that refer to elements of vital significance for their state of mind, dreams that cast light on unresolved worries or problems of the soul (*mashâkel nafsâniyye*) they face.

Potentially, dreams that conjure up and present to us our grandmothers are not less than dreams that present our ancient grandfathers. Psychological contexts do not leave out anyone of our impressive grandparents, but "favor" the vision of grandfathers is considered to be of greater importance in tribal societies and therefore bestows on us greater respect. Greater attention is given to paternal elders, and those who meet with them in dreams gain in recognition and social esteem.

An old Hebrew adage refers to a verse in Zechariah 10: 2 that goes as follows:

> "For the idols speak delusion; the diviners envision lies, and ***tell false dreams; they comfort in vain***. Therefore the people wend their way like sheep; they are in trouble because there is no shepherd."

Changing the emphasis implies a contrary interpretation of the self-same phrase; wording it the same but placing a question mark instead of the exclamation mark at the end of the sentence creates a change of negation: — "The dreams talk in vain!" vs. "The **dreams, talk in vain?!**" meaning that they do not. Then the saying encourages us to "***give attention to dreams!***"

> Provided we speak of bad dreams that ***comfort in vain,*** then, yes! Don't give them a second thought! Maintain that they speak nothing but vanity!

However, once a dream imparts hopes for improvement, foreseeing a time in the future of better luck — accept it. A promising vision that pulls you out of a depression, out of a mood that keeps you down, suggests corrections. The conclusion is: "Do not give up hope. Embrace the offer of a better omen. Draw the encouragement it offers." No dream statistics exist. No psychoanalysts measure, sum up to announce rates of positive as compared to negative dreams in clients' minds. There are no methods to measure night sightings by tense: those calling back past events as compared to those foretelling the future. Rather, dreams reflect the states of the human mind; they do not form them, illusions to a good future, an encouraging spirit that compensates a layered spirit, a dream.

A second understanding, a rather positive one, is founded on use of this same saying but ending with a pitch of a question mark:

> In case a dream expression strokes your ego, all you have to do is to read it properly:
>
> "[Do] The dreams speak vanity?!"
>
> The meaning is, of course, the contrary, saying that they do not. [When our dreams suit our mood] They are a serious matter!

The question of what shapes the images we see in dreams and what determines the phrasing of the words we say or are told in dreams remains a puzzle that most people leave unanswered. It is accepted that there is no way humans can control their dreams. Supposing that dreams are in God's hands, that is understandable. In order to affect the kind of visions we experience, some psychoanalysts reckon, we should keep our direction in mind and confront our worries, be aware of what matters in our attitude in relation to others and our daily activities. Changing our relation to the people among whom we live and with whom we deal has an impact on them appearing in our dreams. All that transpires during the daytime and that impresses our awareness is susceptible to being noted in our psyche and eventually showing up in our dreams.

Changes in the people in our social milieu, like changes in the institutions that administer our lives, are apt to alter the frequency, context and form of their appearance in our dreams. Most people sense it and are aware of this quality, but few bother to follow the associations between reality and dream, to fathom the frequency of this truth or try to measure the way it operates.

The cases portrayed above contain dreams that are predominated by archetypes of founding agnates. We present them as the product of a culture whose beliefs influence people to regard as true that the agnatic set up was founded in the days of Genesis. If not for this tradition, we conjecture, this view of the social set up could not have evolved. It is, we claim, an outcome of an inculcated truism. Appearance of paternal sages in dreams, we assume, could not have been contemplated except by means of this specific cultural pattern.

What is the cerebral apparatus that first selects dream images for us and then implants them in our minds is a question so difficult to answer. Our contribution is in casting light on this phenomenon, in the particular anthropological context described. I trust similar patterns exist elsewhere too. Similar cultural suppositions can create them as much as changes in view of the social order can eliminate them. Similar cultural conditions are a precondition that affect people's psyches alike. Predominance of an agnatic social structure (paternal tribes) would buttress a selfsame culture, but not elsewhere I suppose.

The Arab-Muslim conquest spread paternal tribalism throughout the entire Arab Middle East. Associated tribal-bound cultural phenomena appeared in the desert and in rural districts and also in Middle Eastern towns.[68] On settling in towns the different tribes tended to dwell discretely, each in

---

[68] See Ibn Khaldun, 1958 [1377].

a quarter of its own, and mark the inner structure of the urban dwelling as tribal. Though primate cities of the Middle East evolved out of this tradition, with a tribal dictate of the dwelling, small towns to this day, to a large extent, still follow the rules of agnatic ascription, subdivided into tribal residence principals.

While the current principal of town dwelling shows division by financial ability and individual success, allowing the poor and the wealthy to dwell discretely, in the Middle Eastern towns, both the poor and the wealthy of each group of agnates still tend to dwell alongside one another. Therefore most of the ME town quarters are marked by their dominant paternal ascription (Kressel, 1992).

What precisely brings the revelation of old male ancestors to be preeminent in people dreams, or what is the mechanism that first chooses images of tribesmen, then generates the appearance of Sheikhs in peoples' dreams — remains an unanswered question. Only a comparative study of social life outside of agnatic guidelines, once the relevance of paternal forefathers to their offspring declines, may provide an answer for this question.

While no one can claim conscious control of forming the kind of the dreams one has, the flow of dreams and their meaning are indirectly influenced by our conscious experience (Ogdan, 2005). Predicaments in our way, as well as confusing experiences that occur and leave a deep impression, pave a way for dream events. By impressing our psyche, in the sense of "leaving a scratch," it has an impact on our everyday thinking and an effect on our potential dreams. Changes among acquaintances and our changes towards them affect the potential of our dreaming. We cannot modify the products of "our system," not by directly addressing our psyche. Noticing the consequences of things we do and readjustments we make in reference to other people who have in impact on our psyche shows up in dreams. Problems, uneven events and people in shifting positions we face, that challenge our routine and the conventions on which we rest, may shape the product of our dreams anew.

Daily affairs, routine engagement with people and current attitudes individuals have as regards the world around them rarely explain archetypal dreams. Studies of dream phenomena following psychoanalysts' research, since the late 19th century, have taught of the subdivision and kinds of dreams. This allows us to see a variegated range of causes that provoke the process of dreaming in different ways. Our study points to a cultural agreement, formed along with the living in light of the agnatic social formation, that brings to light and to dreams the images of forefathers.

Among folks living in a social milieu of paternal tribes who adhere to the agnatic frames of thinking and to the social order that stems from them the likelihood of archetypal dreams in which old grandfathers are preeminent increases. Paternal grandfathers who are expected and are welcomed by dreamers come close to the ideal image of traditional tribes' Sheikhs.

To conclude this study we speculate that readjustment of attitudes among tribal folks, following their urbanization, is not necessarily within sight. Migration out of deserts does not affect them, nor does living in town. No basic truism provided in urban life obliges tribesmen to question anew their societal bonds and elements of tribalism. The confines of tribal realism and subdivision of ascription may last and in fact do last in Middle Eastern towns. Along with the enduring trust in tribal realism trust in Sheikhs who represent them does as well.

An old Sheikh visiting in dreams is an ideal and an esteemed experience, ancient and long sought after, believed to be a sign of the chosen among people living in the Middle East. The appearance of a long deceased Sheikh passing through a person's mind while he is asleep is largely viewed as a sign of respect. Sheikhs are believed to be a reminder to their offspring of what "the tribe" used to be and ought to be. As such they evoke awareness of the unity of being called to the tribal flag, voicing the desire to shake free of individualism, to sacrifice oneself for the collective cause. There is no hint of sex attached to the Sheikhs' image. Their image once appearing in a dream is a call for unity, for discipline and sacrifice, rather than anything sexual. They appear to accentuate the importance of a common tribal cause. As opposed to new trends to disregard tribes or dismantle of traditional frameworks, the Sheikhs stand for retaining the tribal framework.

BIBLIOGRAPHY

No name (1960). *The Teaching of Buddha*. Tokyo: Koaido Printing.

No name (1999). *Srimad Bhagavadgita*. Gorakhpur: Gita Press.

Bar Zvi, S., Aref Abu Rabi'a & G. M. Kressel (1998). *The Charm of Graves; Mourning Rituals and Tomb Worshipping Among the Negev Bedouin* (Hebrew). Tel Aviv: Ministry of Defense.

Benedict, Ruth F. (1923). The Concept of the Guardian Spirit in North America. *American Anthropologist* memoir No. 29.

— (1934). *Patterns of Culture*. Boston: Houghton Mifflin.

Blechner, M.J. (2001). The Clinical Use of Countertransference Dreams. *The Dream Frontier*. London: The Analytic Press. Ch. 18.

Child, V. Gordon (1936). *Man Makes Himself*. London: Watts and Co.

Delaney, Carol. (1987). "Seeds of Honor, Fields of Shame". In Gilmore D. (ed.) *Honor Shame and the Unity of the Mediterranean*. American Anthropological Association. 22. Washington DC, pp. 35-48

Durkheim, Emile (1964 [1893]). *The Division of Labor in Society.* The Free Press of Glencoe.

Eph'al Israel. (1983). *The Ancient Arabs: Nomads on the Borders of the Fertile Crescent 9th - 5th Centuries B.C.* The Magnes Press

Erikson, E. H. (1954). The Dream Specimen of Psychoanalysis. *Journal of the American Psychoanalytic Association* 2: 5-56.

Evans-Pritchard E. E. (1937). *Witchcraft, Oracles and Magic among the Azande.* Oxford: Clarendon Press.

Freud, Sigmund (1953 [1900]). *The Interpretation of Dreams.* The Standard Edition of the Compete Psychological Works of Sigmund Freud. Vol. 4-5. London: Hogarth Press.

Goffman, Erving (1958). *Characteristics of Total Institutions.* Garden City, N.Y.: Anchor Books.

Goldberg, Illy, & Bosmat Admon (2003). *The Giant Dictionary for Dreams' Interpretation.* Hod Hasharon, Israel: Astrolog Publishing House (Hebrew).

Greenson, R. (1970 [1993]). The Exceptional Position of the Dream in Psychoanalytic Practice. In S. Flanders (ed.), *The Dream Discourse Today.* London: New Library of Psychoanalysis, pp. 64-88.

Grotstein, J. (2000). *Who is the Dreamer Who Dreams the Dream?* Hillsdale, N.J.: The Analytic Press.

Ibn Khaldûn (1958 [1377]). *The Muqaddimah: An Introduction to History.* Bollingen Series XLIII. Princeton: Princeton University Press.

Jung, Carl Gustav (1953-1979). *The Collected Works*. Bollingen Series XX. Princeton: Princeton University Press.

— (1933). *Modern Man in Search of a Soul*. New York: A Harvest Book.

— (1933). *New Introductory Lectures on Psychoanalysis*. New York: W. W. Norton and Company.

— (1972 [1959]). *Four Archetypes; Mother; Rebirth; Spirit; Trickster*. London: Routledge & Kegan Paul.

Kantrowitz, J. (2001). A Comparison of the Place of Dreams in Institute Curricula Between 1980-1981 and 1998-1999. *Journal of the American Psychoanalytic Association* 49: 985-997.

Khan, Mas'ud (1989 [1993]). The Use and Abuse of Dream in Psychic Experience. In S. Flanders (ed.), *The Dream Discourse Today*. London: New Library of Psychoanalysis, pp. 91-99.

Kluckhohn, Clyde (1962). *Culture and Behavior*. New York: The Free Press. Chapter 22, On Navaho Dreams.

Kressel, Gideon M. (1992). *Descent Through Males*. Wiesbaden: Otto Harrassowitz.

— (1996). *Ascendancy Through Aggression; The Anatomy of Blood Feud among Urbanized Bedouins*. Wiesbaden: Harrasowitz Verlag.

— (2001). Let Palestine Return to Khaybar. In A. Paul Hare & G.M. Kressel (eds.), *Israel as Center Stage; A Setting for Social and Religious Enactments*. Westport, Conn.: Bergin & Garvey, pp. 165-187.

— (2003). *Let Shepherding Endure: Applied Anthropology and the Preservation of A Cultural Tradition in Israel and the Middle East*. Albany: State University of New York Press.

— (2014). Together with Sasson Bar-Zvi & Aref Abu Rabi'a. *The Charm of Graves*. Sussex: Sussex Academic Press.

Lee, S.G. (1958). "Social Influences in Zulu Dreaming." *Journal of Social Psychology* 47: 265-283.

Meeker, Michael E. (1989). *The Pastoral Son and the Spirit of Patriarchy; Religion, Society, and Person Among East African Stock Keepers*. Madison: University of Wisconsin Press.

Neumann, Erich (1955). *The Great Mother; An Analysis of the Archetype*. Bollingen Series XLVII, Princeton: Princeton University.

Ogdan, T. (2005). *This Art of Psychoanalysis: Dreaming Undreamt Dreams and Interrupted Crises*. London and New York: Routledge.

Quinodoz J. M. (1999). Dreams that Turn Over a Page: Integration Dreams with Paradoxical Regressive Content. *International Journal of Psychoanalysis* 80: 225-238.

Roheim, Géza (1932). Psycho-analysis of Primitive Cultures Types. *International Journal of Psych-analysis*, XIII; 1-221.

— (1947). "Dream Analysis and Field Work in Anthropology." In *Psychoanalysis and Social Sciences*. New York: International Universities Press, pp. 87-130.

— (1950). *Psychoanalysis and Anthropology*. New York: International Universities Press.

Sahlins, Marshall D. (1961). The Segmentary Lineage — An Organization of Predatory Expansion. *American Anthropologist* 63: 322 - 345.

Shulman, D., & Stroumsa, G. (1999). *Dream Cultures: Explorations in the Comparative History of Dreaming.* Oxford: Oxford University Press.

Smith, W. Robertson (1889). *Lectures on the Religion of the Semites.* New York: D. Appleton & Co.

— (1903). *Kinship and Marriage in Early Arabia.* A & C. Black. Ltd. Reprinted in Boston: Beacon Press.

Stanner, W. E. H. (1956). The Dreaming. In T.A. G. Hungerford (ed.), *Australian Signpost.* Melbourne: F. W. Cheshire, pp. 51-65.

Tapper, Richard (ed.) (1983). *The Conflict of Tribe and State in Iran and Afghanistan.* London: Croom Helm.

Wallace, Anthony F. C. (1958). Dreams and the Wishes of the Soul: A Type of Psychoanalytic Theory among the Seventeenth Century Iroquois. *American Anthropologist* 60: 234-248.

INDEX

Printed in the United States
By Bookmasters